Wicked
SPOKANE

Wicked
SPOKANE

Deborah Cuyle

The
History
PRESS

Published by The History Press
Charleston, SC
www.historypress.com

First published 2022

Manufactured in the United States

ISBN 9781467151818

Library of Congress Control Number: 2022939453

CONTENTS

PREFACE

I hope readers will enjoy immersing themselves in the wicked history of old Spokane. Out of all the towns I have written about, Spokane is one of my favorites! The city is so rich in history; one is always discovering new things. Hidden historical figures and bizarre stories constantly emerge from timeworn newspaper articles.

As always with my books, I try to incorporate as many true historical facts, full names and dates as possible for each story. I feel this brings the characters to life and makes learning about the town more interesting. Many of my readers tell me they really enjoy learning about the towns' histories while reading about the local pioneers—their personal troubles, fears and accomplishments. With these genuine stories, I hope to bring many of the local citizens, sneaky criminals and vigilantes, ladies of the night, barkeeps, hotel owners, bankers, politicians and everyone in between back to life on these pages. Otherwise, some of these people would be leaving no memories of themselves at all—except maybe a crumbling tombstone or an unmarked grave.

I have great interest and an extreme respect for the early pioneers, combined with a personal fascination with local history and old buildings. I love reading about the first settlers of a town—everyone from the Native tribes, to the soldiers, to the immigrants, to the shopkeepers.

When I look at time-worn brick buildings or century-old hardwood floors, I try to imagine the thousands of people who once visited these buildings. I think of the strong horses that once pulled wagons and

Hardworking unidentified men pause for a minute to pose for a photograph while working on the new sewer line for Spokane in 1915. *Courtesy of Washington State Archives.*

goods down the muddy streets. I think of the gunslingers and outlaws, the bartenders and store owners—all of them living their lives and going about their business, just as we all do today. The saloon named Durkins at 121 Howard Street was the place to go for five-cent Anheuser-Busch beer or ten-cent whiskey shots. Miss Nellie McFadden was the proprietress of the Fern who furnished clean rooms in 1907 at 7½ Wall Street. The local blacksmith, Charles Staley, could fix up your horse's hooves. Some of the local Spokane millionaires were Senator Turner, D.C. Corbin and his son Austin Corbin, Charles Sweeney and his son-in-law Francis Finnucane, F. Lewis Clark, D.G. Russell, Amasa Campbell…

Many of the stories in this book were pulled out of old newspapers, recapturing early Spokane's fascinating history and unique characters. The book is not intended to be a nonfiction project because even after hundreds of hours hunched over, reading and researching articles, I still found conflicting dates and inconsistent historic details, so please take it for what it is and just enjoy the read. This is ultimately a book about the many mischievous and wicked people and the interesting history of early

Spokane, Washington. These true tales all actually occurred in the city of Spokane. This book complements my *Murder & Mayhem in Spokane* and *Ghosts and Legends of Spokane* books with new subjects and stories, so grab them all and immerse yourself deep into the history of this fascinating and sinful city.

So, sit back with a glass of wine or cup of coffee and enjoy reading *Wicked Spokane*!

ACKNOWLEDGEMENTS

There are many people to thank for this endeavor, and without their help and guidance, this book would not have been possible. My wonderful editor, Laurie Krill, has been such a pleasure to work with on my Spokane books, along with all of the other incredible people at Arcadia Publishing and The History Press. Their mission to promote local history is passionate and infectious, and I am blessed to create my many books with them. Their dedication to recording local history is nothing less than amazing, and without them, many books would never be written.

My appreciation is extended to all those individuals who took the time to share local records and documents; without them, this book would not have the extra flair that I love so much.

And, as always, I want to thank every single person who does what they can to preserve history, whether it is volunteering at their local historical society, maintaining old cemeteries and gravestones that would otherwise be neglected or simply researching their private genealogy through sites like www.ancestry.com and www.findagrave.com. In this fast-paced and high-tech world, the past can, unfortunately, be easily forgotten, and every effort to maintain and record valuable data, photographs, diaries, documents and records is of the upmost importance for future generations.

I also want to thank everyone at Arcadia Publishing and The History Press, my family, followers and friends who have supported my writing craft all these years.

INTRODUCTION

The history of Spokane, Washington, is so full of reckless murders and ridiculous crimes that every front page of the local newspapers includes some sort of homicide or wrongdoings lurking between the lines. Stories of hundreds of the messy details of violent offenses and sinister dealings literally take over the town's past. In fact, the judges of nearby towns used to give criminals the choice between going to their local jail *or* disappearing to Spokane! Of course, the convicts always took the free train ride to their nearby freedom.

The city of Spokane started out as a few tents, a trading post and a sawmill around 1870, and it was called Spokan Falls (no *e*). Soon it was platted by James Glover on February 13, 1878, when the town was made up of a half dozen log cabins and a few more buildings and stores. The "Father of Spokane," Glover came to the area after two rough days in the bitter cold. In 1883, Spokane was basically still a lawless town with no government or strict rules. There was not more than five thousand people living in the state at this time. Most of the prairies were home to the local Indians. In 1891, the city chose to change its name to Spokane.

In early 1910, the population of Spokane was only 36,000. With the nationwide announcements of profitable silver mining and excellent business opportunities, Spokane's population soon shot to over 100,000. It attracted a cluster of rich men and was considered the "wealthiest city in America," with over 20 millionaires (and 28 half-millionaires) living there. But with all this financial glory came dreadful consequences. Violent and

LOANED BY MISS E.A. SMITH
NIECE OF MR. GLOVER

THE FATHER of SPOKANE IS HERE SHOWN
AS HE APPEARED ON THE DAY OF ARRIVAL
AT THE COUNTY SEAT - UP AT COLVILLE - AFTER
A HARD AND TIRESOME TWO DAYS JOURNEY
OVER SNOW COVERED TRAILS IN BITTER COLD,
WHERE HE FILED THE PLAT OF SPOKANE'S
FIRST TOWNSITE - FEB.13.TH 1878
MR. GLOVER HAS BEEN FOREMOST IN ALL
MOVEMENTS THAT TENDED TOWARD THE BEST
INTERESTS OF SPOKANE, EVER WILLING AND READY
TO AID AND ASSIST - LIBERALLY ADVANCING BOTH
HIS TIME AND HIS MONEY TO MAKE THIS THE
FINE CITY THAT WE HAVE TODAY
WE ARE PROUD of our FIRST CITIZEN
MAY HIS YEARS BE MANY AND FILLED WITH PEACE
HE HAS THE GOOD WILL AND BEST WISHES OF THOUSANDS.

JAMES NETTLE GLOVER
AS HE APPEARED IN 1878
REPRODUCTION FROM AN
OLD PHOTOGRAPH BY
M-ART-IN

Left: A wonderful view of the Spokane River and Falls in 1881, when Spokane was still in its infancy. *Courtesy of the Spokane Public Library, Teakle Collection, G.M. Bechtal, Northwest Room.*

Opposite: A portrait of James N. Glover in 1878 with a beautiful handwritten dedication by his loving niece. *Courtesy of Spokane Public Library, Northwest Room.*

unsolved murders, reckless disputes, vicious scandals and hushed suicides were commonplace for Spokane.

The following are some interesting and sordid Spokane pastimes:

- Spokane's Chinatown, also called Trent Alley, was overrun by illegal activities such as gambling, prostitution, opium dens and bootlegging.
- The hidden tunnels under the city promoted all sorts of misdeeds and secret crimes.
- Countless murders and corruption occurred, stemming from unthinkable crimes and an immoral police department.
- Craziness came along with the building of the railroads, logging and mining, bringing immigrants from as far away as Finland.
- Bribery, absurd jailings, robberies, countless houses of ill repute, home-brewed whiskey and prostitution cribs filled the buildings and streets of Spokane.

These and many more Spokane crimes, unlawful activities and mysterious goings-on are to be discovered in *Wicked Spokane*!

Chapter 1

PROSTITUTION AND HOUSES OF ILL REPUTE

A more sweeping measure, short of absolutely driving all lewd women from the city, could scarcely be devised. The nine block area is not merely the heart of Spokane's toughest districts; it is practically the entire "scarlet belt." Shut up the houses of ill-fame within these limits and those that remain would hardly be worth counting at all.
—Spokane Chronicle, *December 16, 1897*

Spokane invited the wealthy and elite crowd to come and enjoy prosperity within its city's streets and to build fantastic mansions and attend grand balls. It was well known that when you made your first million dollars, you would hire the best architect in town, Kirtland Cutter, to build you and your family a mansion in Spokane.

But Spokane was also riddled with violence, prostitution and lots of lawlessness. The city was getting pressure to clean up the streets so that newcomers would feel better about raising a family in Spokane.

Mayor Glover tried to clean up early Spokane by creating an ordinance that was officiated around 1884 to discourage prostitution in the city. He wanted all the bawdy or disorderly houses and the girls of ill fame who worked in them to stop all gross activity. If one was found running a brothel or participating in selling sex, it would be a $100 fine and/or six months in jail. He was not fooling around (no pun intended). But the laws did not do much to deter these sexual escapades because they were almost impossible to enforce. By 1888, cribs and "female boardinghouses" lined the streets of Spokane. The police had other motives for debating the spreading out of the prostitutes. If they were centralized, it was easier to watch them and even protect them.

Much later, Police Chief Sullivan routinely allowed houses of ill fame to be open. It was stated that more houses of prostitution were opened and allowed to run under Sullivan and Mayor Pratt than ever before in the history of Spokane. Sometimes sixty girls were put in jail in a day for soliciting sex. A notorious Black prostitute who called herself Marie Taylor was allowed to continue to run her "lodging house" over the Minneapolis Bar while in jail.

James N. Glover, the "Father of Spokane," taken in 1899. He filed the first town site plat on February 13, 1878. *Courtesy of Joseph D. Maxwell, Spokane Public Library, Northwest Room.*

A French Prostitute and a Crushed Skull

One French lady of the night, Martha Delanoy (real name Marie Jeanette De Pape), was brutally beaten to death in her crib at 323 Front Avenue. Her throat was slashed and her skull badly crushed.

On June 21, 1898, Martha's husband, John Saillard, came home after a long night of playing pool at the Echo Saloon. When he arrived, he quickly noticed his wife's bloody body. Frantic, he ran back to the Echo to get help. Louis Bertonneau, proprietor of the Echo, beckoned for the police.

Soon Captain Coverly and Chief Warren arrived at the scene. The crib had been torn apart, as if the attacker was looking for something. The brutality of Martha's wounds made the police suspect that she had known her assailant and that he had a personal vendetta against her.

The police began investigating her murder and soon became suspicious of her husband. His clothes had blood on them, and his arms had finger-shaped bruises on them. It was not the first time the police had been called for domestic violence between the couple.

The police had few clues to implicate Saillard for manslaughter: a bloody gas lamp, a bloody knife and a bloody hatchet found lying in the kitchen. Nevertheless, Saillard was handcuffed and taken to the city jail with a

$1,500 bail on his head. His friend Bertonneau came up with the money, and Saillard was released.

The trial began in January of the next year. Witnesses claimed Saillard was at the Echo during the murder. Police told otherwise; of all the times they had stopped in the Echo, Saillard was not there that time of night.

The citizens of Spokane were certain Saillard would surely hang for killing his wife. But the jury decided otherwise, and Saillard was saved from the gallows. After the baffling announcement that he was not guilty, excitement about Martha's murder quickly left the newspapers. Her killer was never found, and the investigation remained unsolved.

Whatever happened to John Saillard is unclear. The only possible evidence of his future was printed in the *Chattanooga News* on July 24, 1918, when it announced he had been sick and slowly recovering. If this is the same John Saillard, he lived his life far from Spokane in Ridgedale, Tennessee.

CHINATOWN'S DISREPUTABLE WOMEN

Mayor Byrne has issued a sweeping order to the Spokane police department to arrest all disreputable women who parade through the streets of the city.
—Spokane Press, *January 1, 1903*

In the late 1880s, the area known by locals as Chinatown kept the local police very busy. The "bad part of town" spanned a section from Howard Street to Bernard Street, then onto Front Street and down to Main Avenue. Chinatown was chockfull of fish markets, hotels, bars, laundries, opium dens, cribs and more. Some considered the area a complete slum and an embarrassment to Spokane. The police conducted nightly raids on the dens and cribs, arresting as many lawbreakers as they could in a good night's work.

In 1904, one of the most well-known slum lords in Spokane was E.T. Daniel. He owned a large building on the corner of Front Avenue and Stevens Street. It was public knowledge that Daniel illegally rented out ten rooms as cribs upstairs for local prostitutes to ply their trade and collected "rents" from them daily.

An unknown Italian man also worked hard at keeping the cribs full. Together, the men wanted to build a larger building on Front Street (between

The Model Stables was built in 1890 and was located at 326 West Main Avenue in Spokane. *Courtesy of the Spokane Public Library.*

Washington and Bernard Streets, west of the livery barn) that could house stores on the main level and a house of prostitution upstairs. The local director for the YMCA was also interested in getting in on the action. (Curiously, Reno Hutchinson, who worked for the YMCA, was mysteriously murdered in cold blood in 1906. Was it because he was involved in this plan?) The adventure was to cost $1 million, and the women were expected to cough up a whopping $5,000 per month in rent!

Even more strange, a Christian minister named Reverend Ransom Smith wanted to participate in the real estate plan. He already owned the largest parlor house in Spokane. Located on the corner of Front and Mill, his parlor was a very active house of entertainment. Odd that a minister would get involved in such a scandal; perhaps the money was just too good.

Half of all the cribs in Spokane during this time were currently located on the Yale Block, and rents were collected from the women daily.

Daniel was fined fifty dollars for his corrupt actions—a drop in the bucket in comparison to the money he was making running his houses of ill repute.

SPOKANE'S FRENCH SEX SLAVE RING

The citizens of Spokane were sick and tired of the parasites that were importing young French girls for immoral purposes. Unfortunately, the police had their hands tied because the gang of pimps were very organized and had developed a very complex team that ran through several states. Even if any of the men were convicted, it was typically on the charge of vagrancy, and they were released on a light bail and back to pimping the next day.

Two of the most notorious and hard-to-convict sex slave drivers were brothers from France, Pierre and Adolph Gouyet, who came to Spokane around 1902. Between the two of them, they hardly had a penny to their names. During the early 1900s, young French girls were being brought to America on the pretense of securing honorable employment. Adolph was recorded telling the naive girls, "Il y a beaucoup d'argent à faire en Amérique de manière honorable," which translates to, "There's lots of money to be made in America in an honorable manner."

His lies could not be further from the truth. Unfortunately, the poor girls were already in the States and could not speak English. The girls would come to America through New York City and be dispersed by the men to big cities like Salt Lake, Denver, Butte, San Francisco and Seattle. Since the Gouyet brothers lived in Spokane, a large number of the women landed in Spokane.

Although the brothers were arrested countless times for vagrancy, Spokane police were unable to gather enough evidence to put the men behind bars and deport them. Soon the brothers were known as the "Kings of the Parasites" by the Spokane police force.

That was, until Spokane detective Fred Pearson went on a mission. He began the complicated and dangerous task of gathering data, names, dates, infractions and many other bits of evidence so that when the time came to arrest the Gouyet brothers, the charges would stick.

In October 1902, after not even a year of living in Spokane, the brothers withdrew their savings from the local bank: $100,000! They were headed back to France with their two favorite whores, Benot "Minion" Duvon for Pierre and Emma "Erma" Vigno for Adolph. They did not know they were being followed by the police. As they prepared to board the steamship *LaSavoy*, they were arrested. But the charges didn't stick. For unknown reasons, the sex trafficking team decided to change plans and return to the States. Hot on their tails, Detective Pearson did not give up hope.

The elaborate National Bank with a beautiful turret and upper bay windows located on Riverside Avenue, photographed in 1888. *Courtesy of Spokane Public Library, Northwest Room.*

Sure enough, while in Helena, Montana, the men put their women to work in a local crib to ply their trade. Again, they were arrested. They were thrown in jail in Helena and awaited federal court to hopefully be deported back to France.

But as usual, the lawyers hired by the ring were Johnny on the spot, and again the men were released. For another two years, the Kings of the Parasites maintained their houses of ill repute located on both Yale and Main Blocks in Spokane, making the men very rich.

In August 1903, Hippolyte Marr sold her half interest in the Surprise Saloon located at 515 Front Avenue to Pierre for $1,500, furthering their strength in town. They teamed up with another notorious sex slave driver named Joe Caton. Caton had a whorehouse at the 1200 block on Main Avenue in town. His most busy prostitutes were two beautiful sisters named Alice and Louise Bouche, both from France. But while Caton drank expensive wine and maintained his large mansion in Paris, the women barely ate and suffered from abuse.

Ed Dufresne joined the ring and opened a house in the lower part of town called the Monte Cristo. Policeman Martin Burns continually tried to secure a warrant for Dufresne's arrest, but prosecuting attorney Horace Kimball would not comply.

He would claim, "Do you see this long list of places? This particular place cannot be put out of business unless these others were also." Apparently, there was "not enough evidence" to do that!

Soon, a man named Napoleon Dufort joined the ring. He had a French prostitute named Belle Smith whom he demanded work for him. He housed her in the Erie Building during the evening and a place on the corner of Sprague Avenue and Post Street during the day. He would beat her often if she did not make enough money for him. In August 1903, Smith had suffered enough. With two black eyes, she escaped him and made her way to the police, where she begged for safety from Dufort. He was promptly arrested but was released on a mere $300 bail.

The slaves were terrified of the Gouyet brothers and the gang. It was known that if they tried to escape, there was a ranch on the St. Joe River in nearby Idaho that they would be taken to, never to be heard from again. If questioned, the men would tell authorities that the girls had "returned to France." This also went for a place they owned located in Coeur d'Alene. The pimps had spies that would watch the girls' every move.

Adolph was finally arrested on August 28, 1906, and was sent to the State Federal Penitentiary in Leavenworth, Kansas, where he became inmate #6174. He did not stay there very long and was back in Spokane within a few years.

The corner of Post Street looking south from Sprague Avenue with Hazelwood Dairy and Davenport's Restaurant around 1890. *Courtesy of Spokane Public Library, Becher Collection, Northwest Room.*

During the summer of 1907, the brothers purchased interest in the Inland Brewing and Malting Company at Minnehaha Park, just outside the city limits. This building was to be used for many drunken parties and the exploitation of his ladies. They installed slot machines, a full bar and a dance hall to entertain the men. An all-nighter raged on May 12, when participants found themselves enjoying ragtime music from an orchestra and flowing booze. It was even disclosed that people were dancing a two-step number to the music—one that was so sinful it was not even permitted at the local Elks Lodge!

Chief of Police Waller told reporters, "I have forced in the city that all public dances be decent." He threatened to close the Minnehaha dance hall at once, but it never happened.

Much to Waller's dismay, problems and debauchery continued at the park when the Gouyets offered an "auction" of girls. They rounded up ten French girls from the Main Block in Spokane to be sold to the highest bidder. Some of the girls sold for $200, the uglier ones for less.

On November 21, 1907, Pierre Gouyet deposited $11,000 into his bank account, alerting police. Sheriff Howard Doak was told of the scheme but neglected to make any real arrests.

Detective Pearson refused to give up on arresting the Kings.

As the ring gained more strength and protection, another couple came to Spokane from Veginone, France. Leon Vacher and his lover, Henriette Yuppe, made their way to town, where Henriette was promptly put to work as a prostitute to support Vacher. Her worried family tried for years to find her. The French Council begged for support from the Spokane Police Department, and once again, Officer Pearson took the lead. Henriette was using the aliases Louise Vacher and Lillian Dubois, but that did not derail Pearson. He located the young girl while she was working in a house of prostitution in Wallace, Idaho, under Madams Emile Veaucamp and Jennie Girard. She was taken into custody and held as a government witness, soon to be deported back to France. Leon Vacher quickly made his way to Egypt and was never seen again in Spokane.

By August 26, 1907, Chief of Police Rice had been pushed to the limits. He was sick of seeing the Kings in town wearing diamond rings and gold spectacles and carrying gold snuff boxes while their abused women were sharing one dinner plate that cost fifty cents to make. He angrily ordered, "ALL women who live in disorderly houses shall leave town by October 1st or be arrested!" He also stated, "ALL parasites [pimps] caught in this city will be put to work on the rock pile instead of being permitted to forfeit a paltry bond!"

Due to Pearson's hard work and attention to detail, on October 27, 1908, Pierre Gouyet was captured and sent to the Federal State Penitentiary in Leavenworth, Kansas, and became inmate #6204. He was out in February 1910 and quickly went back into the sex trade business.

Adolph returned to France.

SPOKANE'S LADIES OF THE NIGHT

Some of Spokane's more notorious ladies of the night were Dirty Dora, Bronco Liz, Irish Kate, Big Bertha, Leah Spaulding, Myrtle Gray and Flo Darling.

Big Bertha ran a theater in 1910 that was located on the corner of Bernard and Main Streets. Before that, she ran her business (competing with Frank Bruno's) on the Yale Block in town. Not much more is known about Big Bertha. Flo Darling was the most politically daring of the group of bawdy women. In 1902, she ran her house of ill repute on Front Street. In 1904,

Unidentified men enjoy libations at Dempsey's Restaurant in 1896 or 1897. *Courtesy of Spokane Public Library, Northwest Room.*

she became entangled in a long and delirious legal battle against an enraged citizen named E.E. Dempsie (Dempsey). Dempsie owned land in town, and he felt her whorehouses were devaluing his property. He filed suit against Flo for damages. He wanted to purge Front Street of all boardinghouses that were sheltering these "soiled doves."

Oddly, there was a Hotel Dempsey located just one block from the Great Northern train depot that advertised to homeless transients offering rooms for only fifty cents per day. Was this the same Dempsey who frowned on the working women?

DORA FALK: SPOKANE'S BAD LADY

One of the more popular hussies was a woman named Dora Falk. She was often written up in the local newspaper for her misdeeds. In 1910, she was behind bars again at the city prison for being a prostitute and a stool pigeon against the police. She was released and promptly sent to the Salvation Army Rescue Home to think about her bad reputation. She wanted nothing to do with reform and managed to escape. She told anyone who would listen that the home was starving her to death. She stole a cloak and snuck out of the institution and back into the free world. But her freedom didn't last long. She was arrested again by Officer Roy Fordyce for soliciting herself on Main Avenue. She was charged with the theft of the cloak by Judge Mann.

Dora ran away from her hometown of Missoula, Montana, in 1901. She later lived at the spectacular Davenport Hotel in Spokane. In 1903, she hooked up with a shady man named "Smokey" John Lennon, who was a barber but hated to work and was always in trouble with the police. He was a freeloading loser. Once, he threatened to kill Dora if she didn't pay the twenty-five cents room and board for the two of them. On October 30, 1903, Smokey was arrested for living in sin with Dirty Dora at a lodging house on Sprague Avenue. He said they had a marriage license, but he could not produce it. Then his story changed, and he claimed he only escorted Dora to balls and parties, nothing more. Lennon's real name was Grinnell. He got in more trouble when their landlord, Mrs. E. Mead, supplied information to officials, stating, "Mr. Grinnell introduced the woman to me as his wife and was heard to threaten her life unless she produced twenty-five cents for him!"

HOUSE OF ILL REPUTE SCANDAL

Young girls seeking honest employment in Spokane were being tricked into becoming sex slaves by employment agencies. The local agencies fell into dishonest business practices spurred by greed. The Peerless Employment Agency at 335 Main Avenue in Spokane solicited fourteen- to sixteen-year-old girls for houses of ill fame. S.J. Bean of the Denver Employment Agency and D.D. Wansley of the Eagle Employment Agency elected to supply girls for immoral purposes. J.M. Noble of the U.S. Employment Agency at 411 Main in Spokane jumped on board to supply girls for a sporting house and dance hall for Edith Edwards in a bordello in Wallace, Idaho. "Under age eighteen if possible," Edwards quietly coughed up.

The underbelly desire for underage prostitutes became rampant in Spokane and northern Idaho. The girls were sold for ten dollars each and sometimes as little as one dollar. A brave reporter named Sara Serl went on a mission, going undercover to expose these agencies to the public. When she interviewed Noble pretending to be a madam who needed girls, he told Serl that he told the young girls, "It don't pay to work, girls. I would not if *I* were you. What is the use of being a drudge when you can make all kinds of money working at a sporting house?"

Some unhappy person tried to kill off C.U. Huck, who operated the Carr Employment Agency, located in the basement of a building on Front Street and Stevens Avenue. As Huck was standing on the sidewalk, a heavy box containing ashes and rocks was dropped from four stories above his head! Barely escaping death, the shaken Huck never did find out who tried to kill him in 1909.

Houses of ill repute were called cribs located in the "Burnt District" of Spokane. In 1910, police were allowing the reopening of bordellos all along Front Avenue. A brothel on 26th Street was not so lucky. The police raided the Manito House of Ill Repute as many times as they could. Detectives Cox, Fox, Hogan and Thompson arrested Agnes Plummer, May Bloom and Lillian Douglas on vagrancy charges at Agnes's house in Manito Park. She soon went out of business.

The Spokane Police Department may have allowed the brothels to stay open for another reason: profit. They, too, were profiting from the girls working. The women had to pay a monthly fine for being prostitutes, and the fines were quite considerable. In 1910, the city was given $1,305 in fines by the working gals for prostitution charges for just two weeks of work. A total of eighty-seven women paid fines of $15 each. Their madam

Howard Street looking south from Front Street in 1888, before the big fire the following year that destroyed most of downtown. *Courtesy of Spokane Public Library, Northwest Room.*

would collect the fee automatically and give it to the police in exchange for staying open.

But not all working girls were lucky in police matters. Leona Smith, an underage prostitute, was arrested in 1903 while she was living in the Abion Building. Her charge? Drinking and consorting with strange men. She was also arrested for disorderly conduct because she drank beer from a *can* in her room!

IRISH KATE AND THE SPOKANE FIRE OF 1889

One of Spokane's more famous prostitutes was a woman named Irish Kate, who had flowing red hair. Her pride was her lovely locks, and she worked hard to keep them curled at all times. She was born in Ireland in 1866 and came to the United States to make a new life for herself when she was just a teenager. She ended up becoming a prostitute instead.

Kate's vanity was rumored to be the cause of one of the worst tragedies for early Spokane: the Great Fire in August 1889.

The legend goes that Irish Kate was a working girl who ran her trade out of a saloon on Railroad Avenue. One night, after a long day of work,

Kate was enjoying her favorite beverage, whiskey and water. A stranger approached Kate offering to buy her a drink. Kate was not in the mood to deal with any more men that evening, so she told the man to bugger off.

As she caught a glimpse of her reflection in the bar's mirror, she realized her flaming red hair was disheveled. Unimpressed by the stranger, she strode pass him and went upstairs to her room. The angry fellow decided to follow her.

In her room, Kate took to heating up her curling iron by placing it against the kerosene lamp glass. While she waited for the iron to get hot, the man suddenly burst through her door.

"I will teach you not to accept a drink from me!" he shouted.

"Get out of my room!" she yelled back.

The drunk man began pushing and shoving poor Kate around the room. During one push, she was backed against her dresser and the kerosene lamp was knocked to the floor. The curtains quickly caught flame. The man decided to get out of there and ran away. Kate, flustered, grab a few of her possessions before fleeing the room herself.

For unknown reasons, probably fear, Kate never told anyone about the fire that was gaining in her room. If she would have, perhaps the fire could have

Riverside Avenue looking west the morning after the horrific fire of 1889 that devastated the city. *Courtesy of Spokane Public Library, Northwest Room.*

been extinguished. Instead, she hid in a building across the street, watching the flames gain speed, and soon the building was up in smoke.

The flames raged ravenously for a stressful thirty-six hours, quickly spreading until the fire completely destroyed all of the business district—thirty-two city blocks. The firemen were not successful due to the fact that the pump station was not working properly and the men had no water pressure to douse the flames. The mayor ordered some buildings to be destroyed on purpose, hoping that this would stop the fire from spreading, but it did little to help the problem.

Once the flames were controlled and eventually stopped, the townspeople and business owners were devastated. A man named George Davis was killed. The estimated loss of property was millions.

The news of the fire spread as quickly as the flames, and soon concerned citizens were sending provisions to Spokane to help people out. Food, clothing, tents, blankets—all poured into the city by trains, coming from all over the United States. But a few councilmen and local authorities took it upon their greedy selves to steal most of the goods for their own households. Sadly, very little aid actually was given away to those in need. The selfish people were caught, but no one was ever actually prosecuted.

Perhaps out of guilt or depression, Irish Kate (whose real name was Kate Barrett) committed suicide on May 25, 1892, three years after the big fire. At age twenty-six, Kate took her own life by drinking a bottle of carbolic acid. Her body was found outside near the Panhandle Block.

THE CARONS' SEX SLAVE BUSINESS

One French couple, Leon Caron (Tireux) and Lucy Caron, were extremely ruthless when it came to running their prostitution ring. They eagerly brought over dozens of young, innocent girls from France or New York City on the false pretense that they would be getting jobs as secretaries or nurses. Instead, they were forced into prostitution. Spokane had a very profitable sex trafficking ring, and Leon Caron was considered the boss. If anyone was brave enough to tell the Carons no for any reason, they would end up dead in a day or two. The police were constantly arresting the Carons for "importing women for immoral purposes." In 1902, Sheriff Martin Burns was busy arresting the Carons for bringing girls into the United States illegally. In 1903 and 1904, the Carons again pleaded guilty to the same charges. Local citizens felt the Carons were the vilest parasites of Spokane. They kept their lodging houses in an area called the Old Dive Division.

One of the Carons' slaves was named Theresa Martini. She refused to work as a prostitute for the Carons or anyone. And with that defiance, no one ever saw poor Theresa Martini again.

An elderly man named Olaf Johnson couldn't find his cat one day. He thought it was hiding under his porch at 14 South Jefferson Street in Spokane. But when he crawled under his dusty porch in search of his lost kitty, he was shocked at what he found under the boards. The remains of a female skeleton were partially buried under his porch! Oddly, the bones had a knife buried with them.

The Carons were immediately suspected of the murder of Martini and arrested again, but this time they were not going to be released. They pleaded guilty, and this time they were both sent to McNeil's State Penitentiary. They were to be held for a minimum of three years. Leon Caron died before he finished his sentence. It is unknown what happened to Lucy.

MINISTER TELLS FATHER TO KILL HIS DAUGHTER'S SEDUCER

In 1904, a family was torn apart and a young girl was pushed into a life of shame by her lover. Herman Smith and his wife had ten children. The oldest, Mona, told her parents that she had secured a good job in Spokane that paid her very well. She began wearing expensive clothes and appeared very fashionable. The Smiths assumed Mona was doing well at her new job, and they never questioned her, as she had been a very good girl—up until now.

Her parents soon learned that the eighteen-year-old Mona had hooked up with a married man who was forcing her into a life of shame. Her father threatened, "I shall avenge my daughter's disgrace by killing Wooley [her seducer], if I can find him! My pastor and several lawyers told me I would be justified in killing Wooley. And I have a revolver to do it with!"

J.R. Wooley was supposedly a private detective and a mining man. As soon as Mona's parents found out the truth about her new "job," Wooley and Mona fled Spokane to Seattle, Washington, and then on to Portland, Oregon.

Her frantic parents begged local police to help them find their daughter and bring her back home.

Officers in Portland got a telegram asking for help finding Mona, and they soon started their search party. She was found working in the worst part of the tenderloin district in the Marion Block by Officers Lister and Shannon. When questioned, she told the police, "I love Wooley and will do anything he says."

Since she was eighteen, they really couldn't do much.

A year later, the couple was spotted in Seattle. Her parents were still desperate for her return. The police decided to arrest the couple on the charges of unlawful cohabitation. Bail was set at $1,000 for Wooley, although he pleaded that he and Mona were "only friends."

Luckily, Mr. Smith never had to kill his daughter's lover and end up in the state penitentiary for her justice.

Prostitute Bronco Liz Kills Her Husband

One of Spokane's notorious soiled doves was Bronco Liz. She has an interesting life story. Her real name was Ione Jane Whitney Skeels, and she was a well-known local dance hall queen and a popular entertainer of the working men.

Liz met her future husband, Charles "Chas" W. Skeels, while he was working with the local mines (while she was busy entertaining the lonely miners in the region). Skeels originally came from Huntingtonshire, England, and crossed the sea in 1871 to make his new life in New York City before heading west. At the time of their attraction, Skeels already had a wife and two children at home, so their love affair had to be kept a big secret. Skeels was so in love with Liz that he enticed her to marry him as soon as he was granted a divorce from his wife. He devised a wild plan to do this: he suggested Liz cut off all of her hair, dress in men's clothing and go to work on his family's ranch in Choteau, Montana, until he could finalize his divorce.

Liz agreed to the strange arrangement, and soon, she became a working ranch hand instead of a nighttime working girl. She continued to work on the farm, with no one the wiser that she was actually a woman. After several months, Skeels finally did get granted his divorce, and the new couple went to Moscow, Idaho, to get hitched on January 2, 1888.

Hardworking miners were actively entertained by Spokane prostitute Bronco Liz before she murdered her husband for cheating on her. *Courtesy of Spokane Public Library, Northwest Room.*

But instead of the romantic honeymoon Liz expected after their marriage, Skeels sent her back once again to the ranch in Montana to "wait" for him. She returned to the farm, but in February, she became suspicious. The new bride had a feeling something sketchy was up in her new matrimony.

A rumor that Skeels was sleeping with another woman—a Spokane actress named Frankie Howard who worked at the Theater Comique downtown—

surfaced. They met often for sex at her love nest in a building known as Actor's Flats at 412 Howard Street in Spokane.

Liz became furious at the infidelity and went to reclaim her husband, but not before getting her hands on a pistol (she had shot him once before while they were in Cascade, Montana). Liz's choice of weapon was a .32-caliber British Bulldog revolver that she had found at a pawnshop. The pawnbroker emptied the cartridge for her safety, but Liz was so determined to teach her husband a hard lesson that she roamed the district until she finally found someone to reload the gun for her.

Liz worked out a plan to trick her cheating husband into coming out of hiding. She called for a messenger boy, whom she paid to look for Skeels and give an urgent message to him that he was needed at home because she was not feeling well. The boy quickly ran around town, looking for the bamboozling husband, but Skeels was not in any of the saloons in town.

Furious, Liz took matters into her own hands. She and the boy traveled over to Actor's Flats to scare her husband.

After much knocking on the apartment's entry by the boy, a very frustrated Skeels finally opened up the door. Disgruntled and irritated at being interrupted in his lovemaking, Skeels left the room and entered the hallway where Liz was waiting for him. Knowing he was caught red-handed, Skeels instantly became afraid of Liz, as she had shot him once before.

He put up his hands and said, "Don't you make any breaks at me—keep away! I'm through with you forever!"

Liz did not listen. She fired the pistol at him, and three bullets entered his body. One went through his left arm and lodged in his stomach. The second bullet hit his right side. The third one secured a spot in his lower back.

Skeels yelled, "Let up firing your gun, Liz, or you will kill me!"

But Liz didn't care if he lived or died. She looked her husband straight in the eyes, and without any hesitation, she pulled the trigger.

The fourth bullet somehow went wayward—luckily for Skeels.

Liz then turned on her heels and calmly made her way out from the Flats, down to the sidewalk and headed back toward home. Skeels, somehow unaware of the extent of the damage she had done to him, slowly followed her. But he didn't get far. Bleeding profusely, he had to stop at a nearby store and sit on the doorstep. A man named D.S. Cowgill heard Skeels moaning and saw the blood, so he shouted, "Some of you, come help me!"

As the blood slowly drained from Skeels's body, a carriage was called. After ten or fifteen minutes, the carriage finally arrived, and the men loaded up the dying man and took him to his saloon. The men carried him upstairs, where he asked to lie down. Soon, Drs. Essig and Parmlee attended to Skeels's wounds, but they both felt the shots were fatal and that he would die soon.

Officer Gillespie made his way back to Liz and told her she was under arrest for the murder of her husband. He kept her restricted inside her residence until Sheriff Gilpin and Officer McKernam could come and haul her off to jail.

The *Spokane Falls Review* noted that she told them, "Of course I won't deny I shot him, but I was driven to it. I was crazy with jealousy! Since I married him, he has never been true. I met him in the Coeur d'Alene mines.…When I heard he was now living with a woman named Alice somebody…it made me wild!"

T.W. Murphy and Thomas Griffits were hired to defend poor Bronco Liz.

The philandering Skeels died from his wounds the next day while resting at his son Alfred's home. He was surrounded by his mother, three brothers and his two children from a former wife.

The trial for Skeels's murder lasted nine days, and the jury deliberated for forty-eight hours. They found Liz not guilty, and she was promptly acquitted for the murder. They felt the verdict was justified by the evidence that Skeels was a "bad man and a danger to the community."

Almost five hundred people attended his funeral, so apparently local citizens did not consider him a bad man.

The *Lewiston Teller* reported on January 2, 1890, that one reporter said, "We don't believe Liz should have been hanged, but she should have been punished to some extent."

Bronco Liz disappeared from society, and her future remains a mystery.

Chapter 2

WHISKEY, PROHIBITION AND BOOTLEGGING

The only difference between the common drunk and the fashionable drunk
is that the latter has the ability to pay the fine."
—Chief of Police Perry D. Knapp

ooze. Keep it legal, you have problems. Make it illegal, you have a whole new set of bigger problems. In 1919, the Eighteenth Amendment to the Constitution was enacted to "prohibit the manufacturing and sale of intoxicating liquors." Then, in October the same year, Congress passed the Volstead Act, which allowed the law to actually be enforced, so the demand for Prohibition agents was at an all-time high. Prohibition finally came to a well-received end in 1933. Many drank booze as an alternative to the often-contaminated water in Spokane, which could carry waterborne illnesses, sometimes leaving the person dead within a short twenty-four hours of drinking it.

The lawmakers of Spokane quickly found out that making it illegal to sell or manufacture booze simply forced society to secretly brew their own concoctions in hidden places. Spokane alone imported over ten thousand bottles of booze in just three days. People were obviously never going to stop drinking alcohol. During Prohibition (1920–33), many mistakenly believed that people would just magically quit booze because it was illegal. But speakeasies—secret places and hidden establishments where illegal booze was eagerly served—grew by the hundreds in downtown.

Just before Christmas 1927, Spokane police officers Clarence Marcy, Roy Fordyce, Harry Alderson and Oscar Haukedahl were proud of their

Above: A group of men holding bones promoting the "bone dry" support of Prohibition, with William Upshaw, a proponent of the temperance movement, at right. *Courtesy of Library of Congress #2016887964.*

Left: A Prohibition agent destroys eighty thousand pint bottles of beer. It was common for agents to dispose of confiscated booze by openly pouring it down the sewers in front of horrified and thirsty booze drinkers. *Courtesy of Library of Congress #88715937.*

During Prohibition, bootleggers and moonshiners would wear fake cow hooves attached to their shoes to shake off police who were trying to find their whiskey stills. *Courtesy of Library of Congress.*

achievement: they managed to close down thirteen bars in just two weeks. They were certainly not popular with the local drinking population by any means. These surprise raids also stressed out the proprietors, as they received fines or even jail time for serving alcohol to patrons.

SPOKANE'S MYSTERIOUS UNDERGROUND TUNNELS

Although most are now blocked off or sealed off, underground tunnels did exist. Some believe the older tunnels were created during Prohibition to support the booze trade. The illegal booze was often hidden in unmarked containers and moved from one building to another through such tunnels. In truth, Spokane's underground tunnels are real. They were used by the city for the old steam boilers and pipes. The last boiler for Spokane was shut down in 1986.

Some underground tunnels have been investigated and photographed. One basement of the building on the corner of First Street and Howard Avenue, a restaurant (now closed) called Underground 15 (formerly Blue Spark), has items in its basement that go back to the 1890s. The former owner believed there were underground mazes and tunnels.

On Main Avenue, a place called Dutch's Music Shop was once a speakeasy. The building has been there since 1915. Murals adorn the basement, where some claim there once was illegal gambling and drinking of all sorts. Prior to being Dutch's, it was Durkin's Bar, with Irishman Jimmy Durkin tending the bar. Later, in 1939, it became Bill & Harry Ulrich's Café & Recreation Room.

Even under the glamorous Davenport Hotel, tunnels supposedly exist. Rumors of a gentlemen's club tell of a luxurious room used exclusively for private parties located somewhere under the sidewalk along Post Street. Louis Davenport himself was supposed to have a huge vault in the basement. Grand marble steps led to the Early Bird Lounge, as well.

The old Coeur d'Alene Hotel (525 West Spokane Falls Boulevard) was also a speakeasy for some time. Remnants of an old comedy club were in the basement, as well. Once a variety theater, it was turned into a hotel by

A common scene in Spokane bars: men openly gambling and playing a game of faro, 1910. *Courtesy of Library of Congress #2003677183.*

Left: A postcard of the beautiful Hotel Coeur d'Alene in downtown Spokane, advertising rates of one dollar and up. *Courtesy of Spokane Public Library, Northwest Room.*

Below: A postcard of the Spokane Club building in 1910. During Prohibition, the building would discreetly hide many fifty-gallon drums of whiskey. *Courtesy of Spokane Public Library, Northwest Room.*

The Coast Guard cutter USS *Seneca* chasing and capturing a rumrunner in 1924. Prohibition agents are examining the dozens of confiscated barrels of booze. *Courtesy of Library of Congress #2006675962.*

Spokane's famous "Dutch Jake" Goetz in 1909. Goetz was a kind man who would often feed people in need. In his hotel, box rustling (a term for women persuading men to buy them expensive drinks) was alive and well. A pretty woman would walk up to a man and say, "Buy me a drink, please." The woman would get to keep a percentage of the profits from the alcohol sales.

Another place where evidence of underground tunnels exist is in the basement of the Montvale building (1001 West 1st Avenue). Built in 1899 for business and civic leader John W. Binkley, eventually it became a single-room-occupancy hotel to cater to the huge number of people flocking to Spokane. In 1899, rooms would rent for one dollar per week or five dollars per month. There was a large mural of the famous jackass from Kellogg, a burro that reportedly found the gold that led to the mass amount of wealth produced from the mines. These tunnels are now sealed up with bricks.

The expansive and impressive Georgian Revival Spokane Club (1002 West Riverside Avenue) was built in 1910 to accommodate Spokane's ever-growing chain of businessmen. There is a tunnel on the Riverside Avenue side. During Prohibition, the building discreetly hid many fifty-gallon drums of whiskey. There was also a women's lounge, slot machines and a bar to keep people happy.

The "wettest" place in town during Prohibition was none other than the town's own city hall. The basement was full of barrels, bottles and jigs of confiscated booze. Thousands of gallons of liquor were being stored as "evidence," but slowly it was being consumed.

People were finding ways to drink, no matter what. One such hidden secret was a spot on a sidewalk where a thirsty patron could slip some money down a magic hole, and in return, a hand would promptly pop up with a glass of booze for the taking.

A HATCHET-WIELDING SALOON ATTACKER

I ran behind the bar, smashed the mirror and all the bottles under it;
picked up the cash register, threw it down; then broke the faucets
of the refrigerator, opened the door and cut the rubber tubes that conducted
the beer. I threw over the slot machine…and got from it a sharp piece
of iron with which I opened the bungs of the beer kegs, and opened the
faucets of the barrels, and then the beers flew in every direction and
I was completely saturated.
—*Carry Nation, prohibition activist*

When Carry Nation entered a saloon, all hell broke loose. The plump, older woman would come crashing through the saloon doors yielding an axe and her Bible and then scream angry words to patrons and barkeeps alike. She would then try to smash any bottles of booze that were perched on the bar. Nation said she was on a mission from God to rescue people from intoxication. She considered herself a "loving home defender" of the temperance movement.

Born in Kansas as Carrie Moore in 1846, she was regarded as a "fearless child." Her father was a kind but penniless man, and her mother was deemed insane. When she became a teenager, she desperately wanted to get away from her gloomy home life. She fell for a man named Charles Gloyd, and they were married in 1867. She soon learned that her new groom was nothing more than a common drunk. Heartbroken and now pregnant, the young girl moved back home and into her parents' house. Gloyd died from excessive alcohol just six months later. Carrie developed a deep hatred for alcohol after what she had witnessed in her brief marriage.

In 1874, she married an older gentleman named David Nation. Soon, she began having visions from God that she needed to eliminate the evils of alcohol and save its sinners. In 1900, the six-foot-tall fearless advocate for Jesus began throwing bricks through saloon windows and at the expensive large mirrors behind the bar. As she broke the glass, she would read scriptures from her Bible and sing hymns. She would shout, "Alcohol is the cause of all evil!"

She gained notoriety and was asked to give lectures all over the world. Her antics grew to carrying an axe that she would use to smash booze bottles, sexy paintings, mirrors and the windows of

The always irritating but influential promoter of prohibition Carry Nation, who would throw a hatchet at the mirrors (shattering them!) in bars to make her point about the harms of liquor. *Courtesy of Creative Commons, public domain.*

saloons. She would proudly boast that she had been arrested over thirty times doing God's work. "Men are nicotine soaked, beer besmirched, whiskey greased, red-eyed devils!" she would yell out to anyone within earshot.

In 1910, her route included the sinful city of Spokane. Chief of Police Sullivan was on high alert as Nation was scheduled to lecture in a tent on the corner of Astor and Baldwin Streets. She told the *Spokane Press* on May 5, "I never can tell when I will clean out a bar room, for I never know till the moment of inspiration to do so comes to me from God—if it comes while I am here, look out. That's all I can say."

She also hated cigars and cigarettes and was known to pull them right out of someone's nicotine-stained mouth. She would warn, "Don't you know you are smoking yourself into hell?!"

Nation made quite the living out of her lectures and bizarre barroom acts. She was soon earning $250 to $1,000 per week to speak about the evils of alcohol in theaters. She also had little souvenir hatchet pins that she sold in the lobby, earning her another $200 per week. Although she was worth over

$200,000, she spent almost all of her money to support her cause and her newspaper, *The Hatchet*.

At the end of 1910, Nation announced that she desired to retire soon from her barroom bottle-smashing career, but she continued to lecture and wreck bars for another year.

During her last stint in Chicago, on December 18, 1911, she roamed from bar to bar, creating a stir. Although she was accompanied by police and was prohibited from causing any physical damage to the city's establishments, she still managed to gather curious citizens as she preached.

Around midnight, she entered the final bar on her route. As she ranted and raved about the evils of alcohol, she noticed a young man serving drinks to a few already-drunk patrons. She approached the table and held up her Bible and hatchet. The young man looked up at her and smiled, saying, "How do you do, Grandma Nation?"

But Nation did not recognize this man.

"Don't you remember little Riley, Riley White, your little grandson?"

"My God! Can it be possible that my grandson is doing the devil's work?!" At this, she threw herself down on the whiskey-soaked sawdust floor and wailed and screamed. A nearby prostitute bent down and blew cigarette smoke in Nation's face. After a few more moments of complaining, Nation told one of her followers, "Take me back to the hotel, I want to go home."

Four days later, she checked into a sanitarium in Leavenworth, Kansas. She suffered a complete nervous breakdown. She collapsed and was bedridden. Surrounded by only her two nieces, a doctor and a nurse, she died of paresis (a condition of muscular weakness caused by nerve damage or disease resulting in partial paralysis) on June 9, 1911.

Her final words were, "I have done what I could."

JAMES DURKIN: SPOKANE'S WHISKEY KING

James Durkin became one of Spokane's finest businessmen and an early self-made millionaire. He was well respected by all, though his quirky and outlandish promotions made one sometimes raise a brow.

Born in England in 1859, his family and thirteen siblings came to America in 1868. At just nine years of age, he ran away from home and landed at his uncle's house in Brooklyn, New York. There, he sold papers and saved up his money.

At age thirteen, he began bartending. He continued to work around town, doing odd jobs. In 1882, he married Margaret Daily in Minnesota and started a family. A few years later, he headed out to Washington Territory on his own, hearing about the silver rush. Again, he worked odd jobs for several years but soon figured out that the saloons in Spokane were paying way too much to have booze delivered by the jug. He believed proprietors could save a bunch of money by moving booze in barrels instead. And he was right.

Soon he was getting rich with his popular and productive scheme. He opened up Durkin's Saloon on the corner of Sprague Avenue and Mill Street (now Wall Street). His bar offered fine liquors and cigars—and no funny stuff! Although he was competing with over one hundred other bars in town, his was considered the most respectable.

Durkin would go on to become one of Spokane's most notable characters, both odd and brilliant.

WHISKEY AS MEDICINE

The government knows it is not stopping drinking by putting poison in alcohol….Yet it continues its poisoning processes, heedless of the fact that people determined to drink are daily absorbing that poison. Knowing this to be true, the United States government must be charged with the moral responsibility for the deaths that poisoned liquor causes, although it cannot be held legally responsible.
—New York City medical examiner Charles Norris,
announced during Prohibition

Duffy's Pure Malt Whiskey was presented to consumers as a cure-all for almost every ailment. The company touted:

If you wish to keep strong and vigorous and have on your cheeks the glow of perfect health, take Duffy's Pure Malt Whiskey regularly and take no other medicine. Duffy's Pure Malt Whiskey tones and strengthens the heart action and purifies the entire system. It is the only whiskey recognized as a medicine and contains no oil. This is a guarantee.

During Prohibition, some patients were being "prescribed" alcohol as medicine. But they could also only purchase one pint every ten days.

During Prohibition, dozens of barrels of liquor and whiskey-making items were confiscated daily. *Courtesy of Library of Congress #89706122.*

A select few doctors were allowed to prescribe alcohol to patients. They needed to use a government-issued and signed prescription form that was to be glued to the back of the bottle of booze (though most people never bothered). They claimed that booze cured such ailments as cancer, tuberculosis, depression, anxiety, coughing, indigestion and hysteria. During the first six months of Prohibition, over fifteen thousand doctors applied for permits to allow them to prescribe alcohol to patients, as it was very good money. Over 11 million prescriptions were given out to people claiming they needed booze for health reasons. One doctor was said to give out 475 prescriptions in a single day. At $3 each, that would have made him very wealthy indeed—$1,425!

On the prescription pad under the type of alcohol prescribed, the physician would often write "spiritus frumenti," which means "spirit of the grain." At the drugstore, the patient would give the pharmacist the prescription and tell them which type of spirit they preferred: gin, rye or scotch. Some people were even prescribed champagne.

Alcohol stimulants are essential restoratives to poor, sickly, suffering humanity. They cause such a delightful feeling of relief to tired nature; such great rest, such splendid dreams.
—*Ebenezer Alden, MD,* Medical Uses of Alcohol, *late 1870s*

But it was a bit of a scam. The patients were forced to pay the doctor three dollars to prescribe the 100 percent booze, and then they had to pay the druggist another three dollars (about forty dollars in today's money). The average person could not afford this. Bootleggers and homebrew became very popular. Crooked doctors sold their prescription pads to bootleggers, and counterfeit pads were also created, adding to the chaos.

During the pandemic of 1918, many believed that alcohol could ward off the Spanish flu that was killing millions of people. By 1919, one-third of the world's population had been affected and about fifty million people died. The army camps were hit hard with the virus, and eventually, confiscated whiskey was sent to the camps to help the soldiers. Doctors felt the booze was a "necessary therapeutic agent."

The *New York Times* announced on July 20, 1924, that "1,347,573 gallons of prescribed whiskey was consumed in one year and almost 1 million prescriptions are being written *per month*." Keep in mind, these numbers are only the documented amounts, not the *actual* amount of illegal booze being consumed. The consumption of illegal homemade brew was really causing problems, including thousands of deaths and health problems. Improper or contaminated moonshine wreaked havoc on participants and would sometimes cause blindness, paralysis or death. The federal government

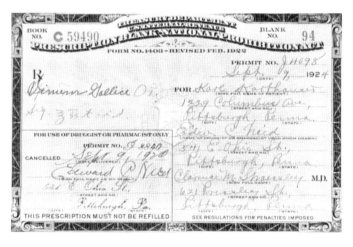

A sample of the pad used by doctors to prescribe whiskey as medicine during Prohibition. They received three dollars for each prescription they wrote, making many of them fairly rich. *Courtesy of the U.S. Treasury Department, public domain.*

Unidentified Americans celebrating the end of Prohibition by guzzling booze right from the barrel in 1933. *Courtesy of the* New York Times, *public domain.*

came to an interesting solution to ward off people from drinking alcohol manufactured for household and industrial purposes in lieu of regulated booze for recreational purposes. They felt that if they added toxins and chemicals to the denatured alcohol, it would taste so horrible that people would not drink it. So in went chemicals such as mercury, carbolic acid, chloroform, gasoline and formaldehyde. But of course, desperate alcoholics plugged their noses and drank it anyway, keeping coroners busy.

Whether booze is prohibited or legal, one thing is clear: people are not going to stop drinking it. The end of Prohibition was a welcome event for a very disastrous and not very well thought out plan.

Chapter 3

SPOKANE MURDERS AND VIOLENCE

Justice has been strangled too often of late, and too many murderers have been dismissed without the infliction of the slightest punishment.
—*Nelson Durham, editor of the* Spokane Falls Review, *1890*

Wherever you have people, you will encounter violence and murder. Spokane's violence grew rampant the more the population exploded. Judges in other cities would give their criminals the choice between being locked in their small-town jails or going to Spokane. Yes, that did happen. And often. Thus, thieves, rapists and other undesirables were quickly shoved off from Wallace, Kellogg, Coeur d'Alene and other nearby towns for the Spokane Police Department to deal with. Completely unfair.

It is a sad fact (even today) that some murders get all the attention and publicity and others barely get a line or two in the local paper. Surely one person's life is as important as another's. Take, for example, the horrible and brutal murder of a teenager working as a stack boy at a farm just outside Spokane. In July 1903, an unknown young man was beaten, robbed and murdered, and then his corpse was dragged to the Spokane River and tossed into a clump of bushes. It was found two blocks below the Monroe Street Bridge by Mat Moore and John Haffton, Spokane locals. Why would someone kill an innocent boy? He clearly did not have enough money on him to warrant being robbed. And why kill him in the first place? But the boy's murder barely gets a mention in the paper, and he was probably buried in an unmarked grave somewhere.

Henry Sample, Spokane's first Black police officer, who served Spokane from 1892 to 1894, with his trusted horse. *Courtesy of Spokane Public Library, Northwest Room.*

SPOKANE'S SERIAL KILLER, BLUEBEARD

One of the worst killers during 1918 and 1920 was a man nicknamed Bluebeard (not the pirate) who killed several Spokane and Coeur d'Alene women, as well as many others. He said his real name was James Watson, then it was Dan Holden, then it was John Gillam. He also used the names Charles Gilham, Charles Newton Harvey, Walter Andrew Watson, Andrew Hilton, Milton Lewis, James R. Hilton-Huirt and William B. Huirt. He used so many aliases that he probably couldn't even remember his real name!

He was a schmoozer of innocent women. This serial killer's modus operandi? He would place a small ad in a local newspaper seeking a wife. His ads often claimed that he was "a gentleman, neat in appearance, of courteous disposition, well connected. Has property and connections with several corporations, a nice bank account and considerable government bonds. Would be pleased to correspond with a young lady or widow. Object matrimony." Signed [one of his aliases].

Serial killer James Watson, also known as Bluebeard, who killed several Spokane and Coeur d'Alene women, as well as others all over the United States. *Courtesy of California U.S. Prison Correctional Records, Ancestry.com.*

After Bluebeard killed Eleanor Frazier, he threw her body into the Spokane River, where it was carried over the falls and then crushed on the rocks below. *Courtesy of the Teakle collection, Northwest Room, Spokane Public Library.*

A beautiful early view in 1894 of the Spokane River and Spokane Falls, where Bluebeard tossed one of his victims. *Courtesy of the Little Art Studio, Northwest Room, Spokane Public Library.*

He would then marry the richest respondent, steal from her and kill her for her money. Meet, marry, kill, repeat. He was a cruel bigamist who murdered a minimum of nine of the twenty-two women he married. He would tell the woman's family that he needed money from them in order to invest in "their" future together. After he killed their daughter, he would continue to type letters and send them to the wife's family so they did not suspect anything. He told his wives that he was a Secret Service agent for the United States government, thus explaining why he would be gone for long periods of time. In reality, he was searching for his next victim.

It was later suggested through his crazy confessions and possible exaggerations that he had actually married over fort-five women and killed over twenty of them!

The following are some of his victims:

- Eleanor Frazier/Fraser, thrown into the Spokane River in Spokane, her body carried over the falls and crushed on the rocks below. He stole $1,000 from her.
- Bertha A. Goodnick of Spokane, drowned in Lake Washington, Seattle.
- Elizabeth Prior, a waitress at the Davenport Hotel in Spokane who lived in Wallace, Idaho. She married the killer in Coeur d'Alene. Later, her skull was ruthlessly crushed with a sledgehammer by him, and then he robbed her of $1,100 in cash and $700 in bonds.
- Mrs. W.A. Watt, who "drowned" in Lake Coeur d'Alene, Idaho.
- Marie Austin, who "drowned" in Lake Coeur d'Alene, Idaho.
- Nina Lee Deloney, struck on the head with a hammer near Long Beach, California, and then buried on a rocky mountain side. Later, he confessed to local police to establish the crime in Los Angeles County so he would get a life sentence in California and not a death sentence in the state of Washington.

- Alice M. Ludvigson of Seattle, "drowned" under heavy logs at the St. Joe River, Idaho.
- Agnes Wilson, "drowned" in Lake Washington, Seattle.

But Blue Beard's luck would soon run out when one of his wives suspected him of adultery and hired a private detective to follow him. She learned that the suitcase he always carried contained women's jewelry and dozens of other marriage certificates. He was arrested in 1920 in Los Angeles, where he confessed to committing multiple murders.

He was sentenced to life in prison at San Quentin, where he died of pneumonia on October 16, 1939. Oddly, he became best friends with his doctor while he was in prison.

THE MURDER OF A POLICEMAN

Roy Fordyce was a well-liked and hardworking officer for the Spokane Police Department in the year 1909. He was so appreciated in the short time he had been working as an officer that the members of the local Beer Driver's Union presented him with an expensive gold ring. He had captured killer Dave Boszell, who had slayed Charles Kemp, a thirty-year-old Black man, in cold blood. Kemp worked in a wood yard at Front Avenue and Browne Street. The twenty-eight-year-old Boszell, also a Black man, worked in Spokane as well. A couple days after Christmas, the two men were near Two John's Saloon. They were drinking and soon began fighting over a woman. At about 10:00 p.m., a .44 Colt revolver was pulled from the coat of Boszell and fired in Kemp's face. Police Officer Fordyce was at the scene, and Boszell pointed the gun at him, too.

"I will kill you too!" he blurted out at Fordyce.

Boszell was arrested and charged with first-degree murder. His trial was set for April 1910.

Detective Roy Fordyce would soon encounter his own killer.

On a cold November night, Fordyce and his partner, George Bradley, noticed a couple of young lads purchasing guns at the local Star Loan Office. Curious as to why the boys needed guns, the officers decided to follow them back to their hotel. At the Spokane Hotel at 414½ West Main Street, Fordyce and Bradley knocked on the door to their room. When the two teenagers, Robert Landis (sixteen) and Charles Dow (twenty), answered the door, Fordyce questioned their motive for needing guns. Panicked, the

Left: Innocent-looking teenager Robert Landis shot and killed Spokane police officer Roy Fordyce, adding first-degree murder to his charges for robbery, violating parole and shooting a drugstore manager. *Courtesy of the* Indianapolis Times, *November 25, 1929.*

Right: Horace Leroy "Roy" Fordyce was killed in the line of duty in 1929. He had served on the Spokane Police Department for twenty years. *Courtesy of Spokane Regional Law Enforcement Museum.*

boys offered explanations. Seemingly satisfied with whatever reasons the boys gave, the detectives turned to leave the hotel.

When their backs were turned, Landis began shooting at them. The policemen shot back at the boys, with one bullet penetrating Landis's wrist, shattering it. Fordyce unfortunately took a bullet and went down.

Bradley tackled the killer and beat him with his pistol until he was unconscious. Dow sat nearby in horror. An ambulance was called for to assist Fordyce, but it would be too late.

Once in the patrol wagon, Bradley asked Landis why he started shooting.

"I don't know why I did it. I didn't want to be caught with a gun and sent away."

"Why didn't you kill me, too?"

Landis coolly answered, "Poor shooting. I couldn't hit you."

Back at the jailhouse, Landis confessed to other crimes. He was wanted in Minneapolis (his hometown) for robbery charges, violating parole and shooting a drugstore manager. The troubled teen was charged with first-degree murder, a crime he did not need added to his list. He was locked up, and his trial was set.

Horace Leroy "Roy" Fordyce (1875–1929) came to Spokane from Ohio and had served on the police department for twenty years. He was survived by his wife, Kilen, and two daughters. Their home was at 3024 West Dalton Avenue in Spokane.

THE TAILOR SHOP MURDER

When Sam Chow (also known as Chow Chong) took on a young Japanese employee named Henry Arao, he had no idea that it would cost him his life.

Chow and his wife, Lucy, had a profitable Chinese tailor shop located at 325 West Main Avenue in Spokane. He needed some help with deliveries and miscellaneous errands, so he hired Arao. But Arao had other plans. He mistakenly believed that he had become Chow's business partner. After a few weeks, Arao became frustrated and accused Chow of cheating him, so he quit. He was determined to open his own shop on Post Street. When business was slow for Arao, he accused Chow of stealing his customers.

Chow was actually trying to help Arao succeed by allowing him to secure goods on credit from his own store. Yet when Arao's debt approached ten dollars, he demanded repayment. This infuriated Arao.

Finally, on December 28, 1904, Arao had acquired enough money to pay Chow back, and he arrived at his shop in a huff. He handed Chow a ten-dollar gold piece, demanded his twenty-five cents change and then stormed out of the store. Chow was just happy to get repaid and thought that was the end of it.

But not for Arao. He had actually been stewing over things for a couple of weeks. The next morning, Arao went to a saloon and drank whiskey and ate breakfast. He then went back to Chow's shop and beat on the door. Lucy, roused from bed at 7:00 a.m., answered the door.

"I lost a five-dollar gold piece here last night when I paid Chow his money."

"You know that store, look for it yourself. I need to make a fire." Lucy proceeded to let Arao look for his supposed missing gold piece as she moved to the kitchen in the back of the store to clean out the ash pan and start the

A postcard showing Post Street in 1913. *Courtesy of Spokane Public Library, Northwest Room.*

daily fire. She took the ashes out to the back of the store. She suddenly heard her husband and Arao fighting and quickly came back into the shop.

Arao was running away, wielding a bloody knife. Lucy summoned the police while Chow lay dying in a pool of his own blood.

The police quickly exited the shop and followed the bloody footsteps in the snow that led them to Sprague Avenue. They were hoping to catch the killer, but he was nowhere to be found. After an exhaustive search, they returned to Chow's shop to secure evidence. Chow was loaded up and taken to the coroner, where it was determined that he had been stabbed fourteen times with a four-inch blade.

When the police began talking to locals in the Chinese and Japanese communities, they discovered that Arao was not a well-liked boy in town. He was confrontational and had an explosive temper. It was also exposed that just days before the brutal stabbing, Arao had purchased a gun, a four-inch knife and dozens of containers of lye. Obviously, he had planned on killing Chow and burying his body somewhere.

Arao was located on January 10, 1905, some thirty-six miles south of Spokane, turned in by a local Japanese man who knew his capture would get him a reward. Police promptly handcuffed Arao as he was scrounging through garbage looking for food. When he was returned to Spokane to be interrogated, Arao pleaded not guilty. He said he knew nothing of Chow's murder. He was thrown in jail until his trial. While in jail, he told the prison guards, "I drink some whiskey and feel very mad." He also confessed to the murder of Chow.

His lawyer tried the temporary insanity plea, but the facts of Arao's purchases of weapons put an end to that. The local Japanese community was asked to gather funding for Arao's trial and appeals, but none were interested in helping out the twenty-eight-year-old killer.

It didn't take long for the jury to say, "We find Henry Arao guilty of first-degree murder."

He was sentenced to be hanged on June 3, 1905. Sheriffs Howard Doak and Francis Pugh loaded up Arao with a couple of prisoners on a train heading to Walla Walla State Penitentiary to carry out their sentences. Around thirty people gathered to watch Arao as he stood on the gallows, awaiting his own death.

When asked if he had anything to say, Arao simply said, "No." The lever was pulled, and Arao swung from the noose for about twenty-one minutes until he was pronounced dead.

Arao would become the only Japanese criminal to be executed in Walla Walla.

The Lloyd Bar Murder

A long night of drinking ended up with one dead on Christmas Eve 1909. Sim Lewis, a hack driver, was arrested for killing his friend Gilbert Lightfoot on a night that should have been jolly. The reason for killing the man was unclear. The two men were drinking at Lloyd's Bar and then left the saloon and started walking down the street. In front of a cigar shop on the corner of Second Avenue and Washington Street, an argument escalated until Lewis hit Lightfoot over the head. He hit him so hard that his skull was fractured. The victim was rushed to the hospital but soon died. Witnesses testified that Lightfoot left Lloyd's Bar on his own and Lewis followed him out into the street, where the two began fighting.

After Lewis was arrested, he was asked if he had anything to say. All he quietly muttered was, "I had no intention of killing him."

After a long-awaited trial, Lewis was found guilty of manslaughter by the Superior Court and sentenced to the state penitentiary.

A postcard of the main entrance of Washington State Penitentiary in Walla Walla, Washington. *Courtesy of Washington State Archives.*

A Christmas Murder

In 1909, the residents of Spokane were hoping for a peaceful Christmas, but they would not get it. On Christmas Day, a couple of Italian men began fighting over some Christmas money. Gamasco Canistraro got into a heated argument with a man named Michele Dagruma. The fight originally started at the OR&N (Oregon Railroad and Navigation Company) freight house on December 24.

The two men would not put their anger aside, and soon knives and guns were drawn. After a bit of a battle, both guns were fired. Canistraro was shot through his side near his heart. Dagruma was shot and his face was flayed from his left ear all the way to the bottom of his chin. A passerby named L.C. Rominger yelled for the men to stop fighting, and they split up and both started running away from each other. Canistraro threw his gun away as he was trying to escape. Rominger chased after Dagruma and grabbed the gun from his hand, but Dagruma kept running. He later turned it over to the police. Canistraro was chased by the police and was captured near McGoldrick Lumber Mill. Dagruma was also captured by police near the Division Street Bridge. Canistraro was not expected to survive. The police learned that the two men were fighting over a couple dollars.

It was a paltry sum that took a man's life on Christmas Day.

Spokane YMCA Secretary Shot in Cold Blood

Reno Hutchinson, originally from Portland, Oregon, was the general secretary for Spokane's YMCA. At just thirty years old, he was shot to death on his way to a meeting on October 15, 1906. His killer was never found, and the motive for the killing was a complete mystery.

He was on the corner of Seventh Avenue and Howard Street around 8:00 p.m. when a mysterious man appeared out of nowhere, raised his gun and fired a single shot that went right through his body. He stumbled into the yard of Spokane postmaster Millard Hartson, fell down a small hill and cried out, "I'm shot! I'm shot! I'm shot!" Then his voice was cut off by the collection of blood in his throat. He died within fifteen minutes.

Nelson Hartson, son of the postmaster, telephoned the police as soon as he witnessed the shooting. "A man has been shot in front of the Hartson residence at 627 Howard Street!"

Charles Rodanight, who owned the Crescent Store, heard the shot and came running out into the street.

The Zeigler Building at Howard Street and Riverside Avenue. The Star Clothing Store and Cigar Shop are shown, and a real estate office is on the right, pictured around 1890. *Courtesy of Spokane Public Library, Teakle Collection, Northwest Room.*

When Detectives McDermott, Briley and Herndon arrived at the bloody scene, they did not have many clues to apprehend the suspect. Footprints of hob-nailed boots (nails inserted into the soles of boots) were discovered nearby in the back of Mr. Chapman's house. When measured, the heel was three and a half inches long, the sole was eight and a half inches and there were twenty-one hob nails attached to the bottom of the boot. The prints ran in the direction the killer fled. The gun used was a .38-caliber Colt automatic revolver.

One witness, Mrs. Hymen, told the officers, "Myself and others in the house heard the shot, but thought nothing of it because there is so much blasting going on now. We heard no one run past the back of the house."

Coroners Witter and Pope examined Hutchinson and reported that the victim was shot at close range right below the heart.

Another witness, E.L. Greer, a traveling salesman, was on Howard Street during the crime and also heard the shot fired. He told the detectives he saw a man wearing a gray suit running across the Hartson lawn.

A third witness said he saw a man in a gray suit get on the Liberty Park car earlier that day.

Police determined that there had been no struggle, as the victim's hand was still clutching papers in it. If he had put up a fight, the papers would have been dropped. When Captain Coverly took a look at the scene, he thought it strange that an assailant would shoot the victim under the bright light of the streetlamp and not the dark, unlit section of Howard Street.

Dr. A.L. Marks had seen two men fleeing from the scene. He saw one man running down Seventh Avenue and a second man running in the direction of Hartson's lawn. The presence of two men would suggest a holdup of some sort. But Captain Coverly still did not believe it was a robbery that took Hutchinson's life.

Other YMCA employees felt the murder had been conducted by an enemy of the YMCA, but why? What could possibly be the motive?

When Mrs. Hutchinson was interviewed, she told the detectives that her husband had been worrying a lot lately, enough to make him lose weight, but she did not know the reason. Reverend "Hindley" returned to the Hutchinson home after the murder to comfort the new widow. The Hutchinsons had been married only two years and had just had a baby six months before the murder. Suspiciously, Mrs. Hutchinson left Spokane immediately after the murder.

The police did not have enough clues to figure out who the killer was. Spokane chief of police Waller offered a reward for information.

A few weeks later, the police got a tip from a couple of concerned people from Rockford, Washington. They mentioned that a man was trying to sell a .38-caliber Colt revolver around town. There had also been a local robbery.

Patrolman George Miles arrested two men who were identified in the Rockford incidents, Frank Dalton and Robert Harner.

Police discovered that Mrs. Hutchinson had been receiving letters from a reverend named "John Masten" in Tennessee, and they became suspicious that she was having an illicit affair with the reverend. Chief Waller had suspected this all along. He theorized that Mr. Hutchinson was killed by a sweetheart of Mrs. Hutchinson's from prior to her marriage to Reno, and now the man was crazy with jealousy.

When they tracked down Mrs. Hutchinson and questioned her as to why she did not tell them that she was "friendly" with Reverend Masten, she didn't have a good answer.

A few years after the murder of her husband, Mrs. Hutchinson quietly married Reverend "Melville Wire" at Grace Methodist Church. Were these three reverends actually the same man?

The world will never know who killed Reno Hutchinson or why. The truth went to his grave.

The "Alaska Widow" Comes to Spokane

Mrs. Georgia Antrium, the "Alaska Widow," was eventually located by Spokane police living in Los Angeles, California. They had been hunting her for months. But she had been buying off inspectors and detectives, so she had kept one step ahead of the police. She narrowly escaped Spokane detective Douglas McPhee by just ten minutes when he caught up with her in Seattle, Washington.

The Alaska Widow had been caught setting her own house on Cannon Hill in Spokane on fire to collect insurance money. She lied and said her house contained expensive furs that got destroyed. She received a healthy check of $1,500 from the insurance company. But there were no furs.

Police Captain Coverly and Detective McPhee had a case against Mrs. Antrium. Tragically, another Spokane police office named Henry A. Stotko, who was a chief witness against her, was murdered.

POLICEMAN HENRY STOTKO'S MURDER

Spokane policeman Henry A. Stotko lived right next door to Mrs. Georgia Antrium (the "Alaska Widow" who was guilty of arson and fraud), and he was actively working up the case against her that would prove both counts of insurance fraud and arson. He could prove she was a swindler and never had any valuable furs in her possession that she claimed were destroyed by the fire.

In 1905, Spokane police officer Henry Stotko was shot in the line of duty during an attempted robbery at Shinn's Commission House on Railroad Avenue. *Drawing courtesy of author, original photograph from the Spokane Regional Law Enforcement Museum.*

Antrium was not happy with Stotko. Stotko had only been with the department a few years before he was killed. Coincidence? Or did Antrium pay someone to kill Stotko?

On the night of April 3, 1905, Stotko was on his way home at 4:00 a.m. after finishing his shift of night patrol. He was walking south on Post Street because he lived close to work; his house was located on Eleventh Avenue. At that hour, there would only be about three policemen on duty now that he was off. As Stotko crossed the tracks at the Northern Pacific Railroad yard, he heard unusual noises coming from inside the Shinn's Commission House at Railroad Avenue and Post Street.

He peered into the dark building. Crouching down were James Dalton (aka Edward Westerman, nicknamed "Piano Red") and three other men. They were trying to blow up the safe. Unfortunately for Stotko, the brass buttons on his new uniform made him an easy target, as the streetlamps made them flicker like lights.

When Stotko interrupted their plans, their lookout man (who was standing on the docks) shot him in cold blood. The bullet entered the left side of his neck and passed through to his right shoulder. The shot paralyzed him instantly. The fact that he became paralyzed was most likely the reason they did not shoot him a second time. The burglars, hearing the shot, came running outside to see what was going on. Then they dragged his body out into the street and over between the docks and freight cars. As the men stood over Stotko's motionless body, one of the men raised his gun and was going to shoot him again. Instead, one of them said, "Don't. He's dead." The ruthless crooks proceeded to rob Stotko of what little money he had on him.

The Northern Pacific Railroad freight depot being built in 1888, located between Second and Third Streets on Madison Street. *Courtesy of William Donahue, Spokane Public Library.*

They also stole his watch and his revolver. Then, oddly, they removed his star badge and placed it on his leg cuff. Then they went back to trying to open the safe like nothing had happened. After a moment, the men decided to run off and not bother with the safe any longer.

Stotko lay in the dark, cold air for what would seem like an eternity, unable to move or call out for help. At about 4:45 a.m., Officer DeWolf was walking past the docks on his patrol. He somehow heard Stotko's muffled cries for help.

"Who are you?" asked DeWolf to the stranger lying on the ground.

Stotko tried as hard as he could to speak and was finally able to mumble a few words. DeWolf immediately called for a wagon, and they carefully loaded the injured policeman into the bed of the cart. The wagon rushed off to Sacred Heart Hospital.

The doctor pronounced, "The bullet had entered his neck below his left ear, passed through the nerves between his esophagus and spinal cord, exiting the top of his right shoulder. The artery in his neck was also severed."

Stotko fought for his life for sixteen long hours. He seemed like he was going to get better, and then, just as suddenly, he quickly got worse. He died at 8:00 p.m. on April 4 with his wife at his side. The physician told her, "He died of paralysis of the pneumogastric nerve in his throat."

When the detectives investigated the damaged safe, they found that the men had poured nitroglycerin into a hole in the safe and then stopped it up with a bar of soap. Two bales of hay were pressed up against the safe, probably to muffle the noise of the explosion and catch flying debris. After the failed explosion and the murder of Stotko, the men abandoned their mission.

Inside the safe? Nothing but a few worthless documents and a handful of papers. Hardly worth taking a man's life.

Stotko was a brave and well-liked officer in the Spokane Police Department. A $500 reward was offered for Dalton, and it was soon bumped up to $1,000. The reward then got bumped up again to $2,566 when concerned citizens of Spokane took up a donation and added $1,566 to the reward money. The reward was claimed by Dalton's landlady, Libby Morgan. Dalton was sentenced to hang on October 12, 1907, for Stotko's murder.

Meanwhile, the Alaska Widow was in Los Angeles claiming she was a traveling saleslady and assumed the name Mary McAllister. She was finally jailed for 120 days for shoplifting.

In 1886, Mother Joseph and the Sisters of Providence founded Sacred Heart Hospital when it had just thirty-one beds. *Courtesy of Spokane Historical Preservation Office and Washington State Archives.*

Strangely, Stotko's very wife did everything in her power to free Dalton. Why? She felt Dalton was innocent when nobody else did. Governor Mead granted Dalton a reprieve of sixty days on the grounds of a flaw in the appeal. Over one hundred lawyers signed a petition to reduce his punishment to life in prison due to not enough evidence.

A witness named Miss Tipton came forward and stated that she, Dalton and a man named Hunt had been across the street from the crime scene at the O.K. Theater the night of the murder. Tipton and Hunt both worked at the theater.

Tipton claimed she heard someone say, "Hunt, that was a fine shot you made. You brought down the bullet." And then she heard Hunt respond,

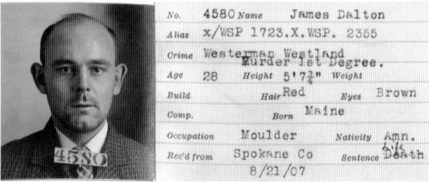

Top: The mug shot of Edward Westerman (aka James Dalton) in 1897, when he was sentenced to five years for stealing horses. *Courtesy of Washington State Archives, Walla Walla Penitentiary records.*

Bottom: James Dalton's (aka Edward Westerman) mug shot when he was arrested again in 1907 and sentenced to death (then changed to life) in 1907. *Courtesy of Washington State Archives, Walla Walla Penitentiary records.*

"Tipton, I do not know if it was my shot that struck him, for he was hit on the other side."

Stotko told what he remembered before he died: "There were two men on either side of me and the men were well dressed." Dalton was wearing grubby clothes—overalls and a dirty sweater—and looked like a laborer, not a well-dressed man.

Dalton told his lawyer, "I am innocent as an unborn babe. I had nothing to do with that murder, but I am a convict and that made it easy for the prosecutor and police." He had been caught stealing a horse on June 20, 1897, and did time in the Walla Walla State Penitentiary. He was released on January 11, 1901.

Stotko's funeral was one of the biggest and most observed funerals ever held in Spokane; thousands mourned his murder.

Mrs. Stotko held to her belief that Dalton was innocent. She told the police, "My husband saw no one until after he was shot and that the men had on black clothes. It was proven by the state that Dalton had on blue overalls and a red sweater."

Dalton went to trial, and after only twenty minutes, the jury found him guilty of murder. He was sentenced to hang at Walla Walla State Penitentiary.

Two Vengeful Indians and the Murder of Officer Robert J. Rusk

Spokane police officer Robert J. Rusk was considered one of the bravest men on the force. Well liked and hardworking, he was respected by all. Well, *almost* all.

Spokane in the late 1800s was a rough-and-tumble kind of town, still considered Spokan Falls territory. The only jail was a small, square wooden "box" that would house criminals.

One night in June 1885, a drunken Indian named Crow Foot was frantically chopping the log walls of the jail with an axe, hoping to free his drunk friend Chimikin. Disturbed by Crow Foot's activity, Officer Rusk promptly arrested him and threw him in jail alongside his friend. Rusk felt it was best for the two men to sleep it off in the safety of the jail.

The next morning, Rusk released the Indians, wishing them to go on their merry way. He thought all was good and the men would return to their normal lives without further incident.

Left: A group of unidentified Indians and cowboys on a dusty trail around 1897. *Courtesy of the Library of Congress #2016653518.*

Below: An unidentified man and two Chinese men riding donkeys while prospecting for gold out on the range. *Courtesy of the Library of Congress #2016817697, by William Henry Jackson around 1880.*

Opposite: In 1886, Spokane police officer Robert J. Rusk rode on horseback to Chewelah (pictured in 1906) for gold prospecting. He was found a few days later dead in Deadman's Creek. *Courtesy of Spokane Public Library, Northwest Room.*

(01-94G-116)(3-27-30-1P.M.)(12-500)
CHEWELAH WN.

But that was not the case. Crow Foot and Chimikin remained angry at Rusk and decided to plot revenge for preventing the jailbreak.

On a sunny day in April 1886, Rusk went on a much-deserved camping trip. He was loaded up with supplies and headed out on horseback to Chewelah to do a little gold prospecting. As he rode across the Third Street Bridge in town, he had no idea he would never return to his beloved city. For the few who watched him ride away, they had no way of knowing it would be the last time they would see their committed Officer Rusk alive.

A few days later, Rusk's newly bought horses mysteriously returned to their former owner's property, both unsaddled and unbridled. Suspecting foul play, the farmer went to the police station to let them know of the strange occurrence. A search party was quickly formed to try to find Rusk.

Sadly, Rusk's body was found by A.R. Junken, facedown in Deadman's Creek. He had suffered a fatal gunshot to his temple.

Horrified, the citizens of Spokane feared the worst. If such a man as Rusk could get murdered, how was anyone safe?

A few days went by with no leads as to who had killed Rusk or why.

Several days later, an old Indian named Curly Jim arrived at the station. "I know who killed your policeman and where his belongings are buried,"

The Spokan Falls area in 1886 looking north from above South Hill. *Courtesy of Spokane Public Library, Northwest Room, Teakle Collection, Northwest Room.*

he told the officers on duty. He also said that the killers had bragged about the murder to fellow Indians.

Curly Jim was paid fifty dollars for the valuable information. Spokan Falls marshal James Gilpin rode out to Williams Lake, where Curly had told him they would find the murderers. Crow Foot was arrested as soon as he was found. A few days later, the arrest of Chimikin followed. Both assailants were charged with manslaughter and received a sentence of twenty years in jail at the Walla Walla Territorial Prison. Both Indians died in prison.

ALMOST THREE HUNDRED WASHINGTON State officers have been killed in the line of duty. Washington is third in line for the most deaths of police officers. We honor with respect these Spokane policemen (of many) who died to protect Spokane's citizens (details of their last days can be found at www.spokanecounty.org/1388/Roll-Call-of-Honor):

- Deputy Sheriff James Joseph Slater, Spokane County Sheriff's Office
  End of Watch: Friday, August 29, 2003
- Sergeant Robbin B. Best, Spokane Police Department
  End of Watch: Friday, February 13, 1987

- Detective Brian Frederick Orchard, Spokane Police Department
  End of Watch: Wednesday, July 20, 1983
- Deputy Sheriff Joseph M. O'Connor, Spokane County Sheriff's Office
  End of Watch: Sunday, August 13, 1961
- Patrolman John F. Wright, Washington State Patrol
  End of Watch: Sunday, June 28, 1953
- Patrolman Ivan Belka, Washington State Patrol
  End of Watch: Saturday, August 18, 1951
- Officer George P. Lancaster, Spokane Police Department
  End of Watch: Thursday, November 18, 1943
- Officer John H. Miller, Spokane Police Department
  End of Watch: Sunday, February 12, 1939
- Game Warden Herbert W. Minnick, Spokane County Game Commission
  End of Watch: Wednesday, October 19, 1932
- Detective Roy Fordyce, Spokane Police Department
  End of Watch: Wednesday, November 13, 1929
- Deputy Valentine J. McDavis, Spokane County Sheriff's Office
  End of Watch: Tuesday, June 12, 1928
- Officer Frederick A. Germain, Spokane Police Department
  End of Watch: Friday, July 21, 1922
- Town Constable Mahlon Pascal Johnson, Waverly Town Police
  Department
  End of Watch: Tuesday, June 14, 1921
- Officer William D. Nelson, Spokane Police Department
  End of Watch: Friday, March 19, 1920
- Officer Michael F. Tynan, Spokane Police Department
  End of Watch: Saturday, June 24, 1916
- Officer Frederick E. Goddard, Spokane Police Department
  End of Watch: Wednesday, March 5, 1913
- Captain John T. Sullivan, Spokane Police Department
  End of Watch: Saturday, January 7, 1911
- Officer Alfred B. Waterbury, Spokane Police Department
  End of Watch: Thursday, October 28, 1909
- Officer Henry A. Stotko, Spokane Police Department
  End of Watch: Tuesday, April 4, 1905
- Marshal Edward F. Whittier, Cheney Police Department
  End of Watch: Tuesday, October 9, 1888
- Officer Ephriam John Hubbard, Spokane Police Department
  End of Watch: Tuesday, September 7, 1886

- Officer Robert J. Rusk, Spokane Police Department
  End of Watch: Thursday, April 22, 1886
- Deputy Sheriff Horace P. Stewart, Spokane County Sheriff's Office
  End of Watch: February 18, 1867

THE MYSTERIOUS DISAPPEARANCE OF SPOKANE MILLIONAIRE CLARK LEWIS

The mysterious disappearance of prominent Spokane citizen Francis Lewis Clark has never been solved.

Clark was one of the city's earliest millionaires, acquiring his wealth through real estate, banking and his C.&C. Flour Mill (the largest mill in the Pacific Northwest). Spokane citizens called him their "Eloquent Entrepreneur." Clark was born in Bangor, Maine, in 1861. He went to Yale University in 1878 and later graduated from Harvard University in 1883. He moved to Spokane in 1884. He luckily purchased a parcel for $900 that was later worth $1 million! He also sold the parcel that the lavish Davenport Hotel was built on for a hefty price and carried the contract for Louis Davenport so he could build his glorious hotel. He invested in two silver mines in the Coeur d'Alene region, the Last Chance Mine and the Tiger-Poorman Mine. These were later sold to the Rockefellers. Clark was an avid yachtsman and won many races with his award-winning boat the *Spokane* and enjoyed his yacht the *Bumble Bee*. He traveled around the world in 1902. After becoming a millionaire, he followed the Spokane tradition of hiring acclaimed architect Kirtland Cutter to build a 14,400-square-foot mansion for himself, his wife, Winifred, and their only son, Theodore. The mansion (now offices for health services) is at 703 West Seventh Avenue. In 1910, they built another 15,000-square-foot mansion on 1,400 acres off Hayden Lake in Idaho. They called it Honeysuckle Lodge.

The mystery begins in January 1914, when the couple traveled to Santa Barbara, California, to get away from the cold Washington winter weather. On January 14, they arrived at the train station together, but soon Clark was kissing his wife goodbye as she boarded the train with their son, Teddy, heading back to Spokane. The train was scheduled to leave at 11:30 p.m. Clark then walked over to his limousine, where his chauffeur, Walter Shute, was waiting. He told Shute that he felt like walking back to the hotel, taking the mile-long walk along the boardwalk to get some fresh air.

A postcard of the extravagant Francis Lewis Clark's 14,400-square-foot mansion, designed by Spokane architect Kirtland Cutter. Clark disappeared without a trace in 1914. *Courtesy of Spokane Public Library, Northwest Room.*

His health was failing, and the warm weather of California was a welcome change. He asked Shute to wait for him overnight and pick him up at the Potter Hotel in the morning.

That was the last time anyone saw Lewis Clark. He simply vanished.

Many speculations about his disappearance emerged, everything from being kidnapped and held for ransom, to suicide, to cold-blooded murder. Rumors that the Clarks had a nasty quarrel right before Winifred boarded the train surfaced. At the time of his disappearance, Clark's estimated worth was $50 million.

The only evidence that ever was recovered was the hat he was wearing the night of his disappearance. After Shute waited around for Clark a few days and his employer never returned, he became very worried. He summoned the police to try to locate Clark. A week later, a body washed ashore north of Caviola, but after investigation, it was found that the body was not that of Clark.

Winifred was told of her husband's disappearance, and she frantically boarded the next train back to Santa Barbara from Spokane. The police believed Clark had jumped off the end of Stearns Wharf Pier and committed suicide. When Shute was questioned, he said there was no way his employer would have killed himself. Mrs. Clark also demanded that it was not a suicide. By January 29, 1914, Clark had been missing for twelve days.

Clark picture from the *Boston Globe*, February 23, 1929. *Drawing courtesy of author.*

An unexpected, anonymous letter arrived at the *Los Angeles Examiner*'s office. The Los Angeles chief of police announced that he had a ransom note from a group claiming to be holding Clark. The letter read as follows: "We are holding Millionaire Clark for ransom of $75,000. State in *Examiner* if his folks will pay it or not. He is well taken care of. Yours, THE BLACKMAILERS."

The police were pretty sure the note was a hoax. Winifred had no problem paying the $75,000 but wanted proof that her husband was alive and well. They placed a reply to the blackmailers asking for proof that the fifty-two-year-old Clark was still alive, but it never came.

Winifred at one point stated that she felt her husband was actually in a sanitarium, or mental hospital, in California, and his disappearance was a cover-up. Winifred's brother-in-law put out a $5,000 reward for the return of Clark alive and $200 for his body. He told the press, "We are unable to disabuse our minds of the possibility that Mr. Clark is in some sanitarium, hospital or even held in duress in this vicinity."

Months passed, and Clark (or his body) was never found.

In June, Detective Bruce got a surprise visit from a woman who called herself Marie Allen (also Margaret Kelly). She claimed her guilty conscience was causing her stress and she needed to confess what she knew about Clark's demise. She said that she was part of a blackmail ring in Santa Barbara called the Spook Trust that focused on wealthy men. Her Spook name was "Clarice the Blonde." She would pose as a spiritual medium for wealthy clients to secure information from them. She would also get rich men into compromising positions to later blackmail them.

She told the police, "I met Clark at the Potter Hotel, where we were later going to get together." She confessed to pretending to be a psychic and to victimizing wealthy people. She was arrested but later released.

The police returned to their suicide status for Clark, and the file was closed.

The case remained cold for fifteen years. Clarice the Blonde again went to the police station in 1929 and told Detectives Sanderson and Romero her version of the mysterious disappearance.

Clark was murdered and thrown into the ocean near Santa Barbara on January 17, 1914 by five men who robbed him. My cut of the money secured from Clark was $800. A Chicago man named "Blackie" paid me $800 for going with Clark by taxi from Los Angeles to Santa Barbara, where a group of five men were going to rob Clark. I was going to meet Clark at Potter Hotel. I did not know that the men planned to kill Clark until it was too late. I did not see Mr. Clark being killed. I drove with him to Santa Barbara, as I have told you, and he left me out at a hotel there, promising to return later. I knew the mob was coming up there and probably would rob him but I did not know of the murder until several months afterward.

She was arrested in connection to blackmailing, robbing and murdering Clark. Once locked up, she claimed it was all a mistake and she had never heard of Clark.

After she spent a few days in the slammer, police were unable to collect enough hard evidence to keep Clarice behind bars. She was released. The police thought Clarice was crazy. No follow-up to Clark's murder or disappearance was prompted, and the case was closed.

Clark left Winifred $700,000 and his son $10. She spent a year in France in 1917 and then returned to Spokane. She lived in Spokane until 1940, when she died at age seventy-one. Winifred tried to maintain the two Clark mansions, but eventually, they went back to the bank. Today, the Spokane mansion is home to offices, and the Hayden Lake mansion was a bed-and-breakfast (now closed).

A rare photograph of Marie Allen, who called herself "Clarice the Blonde." She would pose as a spiritual medium for wealthy clients to secure information out of them and then later blackmail them. *Courtesy of the Evening Capital News, Boise, Idaho, June 16, 1914.*

Now, over one hundred years later, the mystery of Spokane millionaire Lewis Clark's disappearance remains unsolved.

SUICIDE OR MURDER AT THE HOTEL PEDICORD?

Thomas Pedicord came to Spokane in 1889 and began running the Hotel Pedicord in 1895. (It was built in 1893 by millionaire Francis Lewis Clark, who mysteriously disappeared in 1914.) The Hotel Pedicord was a beautiful, upscale hotel boasting 78 rooms, hot and cold running water ("medicinal" water with healing properties from the nearby Medical Lake), intricate iron balconies and a coffee shop and café on the main level. Built at 209 West Riverside Avenue in 1892, the hotel offered short-term stays at a reasonable rate. The fabulous building was designed by the famous local architect Kirtland Cutter with the help of fellow architect John Poetz. Pedicord later expanded the hotel to 165 rooms and ran the hotel until his death at age fifty-seven in 1916.

On February 19, 1903, a good-natured man named James Degnin registered at the Hotel Pedicord around 9:00 p.m. and went straight to his room. What happened the next morning remains an unsolved mystery to this day.

Around 7:30 a.m., Pedicord chef B.L. Rocze went to the cellar to gather items to prepare the day's menu. When he approached the back door, he noticed blood oozing in from the outside. When he opened the door, he was shocked to see the bloody body of James Degnin, who had apparently fallen out of one of the rooms' windows. In fact, he had come from the third-floor window above from room no. 54. Degnin's body had crashed on the rocks at the east corner cellar door entrance to the Hotel Pedicord.

Rocze immediately notified the police. Degnin's body was still warm when they arrived, suggesting he had come out the window just minutes before the chef found him. Degnin's body was removed and taken to the morgue.

Top: A postcard of the Hotel Pedicord located on Riverside Avenue, where the body of James Degnin was found in 1903. The mystery of his murder, suicide or accident was never solved. *Courtesy of Spokane Public Library, Northwest Room.*

Bottom: Drawing of Spokane's famous architect Kirtland Cutter (1860–1939), who designed hundreds of elegant homes and buildings in Spokane. *Courtesy of author.*

Initially, the police thought Degnin had died by suicide, but when they inspected his room, there was no suicide note found nor any other clues that would implicate that he wanted to kill himself. He showed no signs of depression or anxiety when he had checked in the night before; in fact, he was in a jolly mood.

Next, the detectives wondered why Degnin was clad only in his underwear. Certainly someone who was going to plunge to his death from a window would not remove his clothes first.

After their investigation, the police were left with more questions than answers. Did someone push Degnin out the window? If so, who and why? The windows only opened from the bottom up, and it would be pretty hard for an intruder to force Degnin out the window. Was he with a woman and a jealous husband caught them together? But there was no sign of a struggle inside room no. 54.

They wondered if possibly he had opened the window for fresh air, somehow lost his balance and fell from the third floor. But if this was the case, he would have had to actually lean out the bottom half of the window (without the iron balconies), which would make it pretty hard to fall out of. The chances of Degnin being drunk at 7:30 a.m. seemed unlikely as well.

James Degnin's mysterious and bizarre death at the Hotel Pedicord remains unsolved.

Strange Son Sidney Slays Father over Twenty-Five Dollars

If I had to do it all over again, I would still kill him.
—Sidney Sloane, as told to his cell mate, R.A. Mitchell,
about murdering his father

Every front page of the *Spokane Press* during 1906 had some headline or another about the horrific slaying of James "Jim" Sloane by his "insane" teenage son. The trial captured everyone's attention, as it was so gruesome some Spokane citizens were having a hard time even believing it.

Sidney (just a seventeen-year-old boy at the time) and his father were fighting one evening. After a bit of arguing, Sidney lost his temper. His dad had been drinking again and was talking ill of Sidney and his mother.

Sidney loved his mother very much, and his patience for his father's abuse was wearing thin.

Just one day before the murder, Sloane had taken Sidney into his office and proudly introduced him to his fellow workers. He seemed proud of him. Everyone in the office was happy to see such a good father/son relationship. But the next morning, when they opened the *Spokane Press* and read about their boss's brutal murder, they were surprised and in utter shock. What in the world could have happened to cause such a brutal crime?

Sloane's bloody body was discovered in the alley behind their family home at 513 Sixth Avenue, on the corner of Sixth Avenue and Stevens Street. That morning, Mrs. James Petty, who lived next door, looked out her window to see a man lying in the alley. She figured it was just a drunk and almost gave it no attention.

Later, Mrs. Petty told her story to the officers:

> *I had risen at 3:45 a.m. in order to do the family washing before the heat of the day. A few minutes later, I noticed a man's foot in the alley, and next my attention was attracted by a young man waving for me to come downstairs. He told me that a drunken man was lying in the alley. When I went and checked, I found blood on the man's left hand and saw that he was dead. A wallet lay on his breast and papers from his pocket were strewn about the body.*

The Spokane police quickly arrived at the scene to investigate the body of the dead man. Through the gashes and blood, they still recognized the victim as Sloane. He had a bloody towel wrapped around his head.

The police officers walked over to the Sloane house and knocked on the door. Sidney answered the door slowly. The officer held up the blood-soaked rag, and Sidney started crying.

"Better shape up," said Sergeant McPhee, coldly.

"Where is he?" asked the boy, pretending he didn't know the whereabouts of his father.

"Let's go see," McPhee said and took him to the back alley, where the bloodstained corpse was still lying. Sidney sank to his knees and began crying again.

"Better go and find your mom," the officer said. Sniffling, Sidney told the cop that his mother was off camping out by Nine Mile Bridge with his brother. The officer felt an overwhelming sense of pity for the boy, kneeling next to the hacked-up corpse of his father. Until…

When Sidney stood up and faced McPhee, he saw that the boy had not really been crying. It was all for show. Not a single tear had really been shed. That was when McPhee knew he had his killer.

The coroner came to remove the body while several other officers worked the crime scene.

Under the porch of the Sloane house, they found a bloody axe, a piece of bloody carpet and bloody rags. Inside, the remaining carpet and walls told the gruesome tale of the last harrowing moments of James's life. The bloody, smeared footprints in the living room proved that Sloane had obviously been trying to get away from his assailant. Spatters of blood, all on the high ceiling, suggested that the blows from the axe came down with great anger and strength.

Sidney was quickly arrested by Detective McDermott, on orders from McPhee, but he tried to pin the crime on a stranger named Riley. The officers found fifty blood-soaked dollar bills in the boy's pockets.

As the teenager sat in the interrogation room, he refused to talk. For a long time, he just stared at the floor and remained silent. But when the investigators mentioned Sidney's mother, he broke down crying and began to talk.

"My dad had come home drunk again, and we began arguing. I wanted to rob my dad, I dunno why."

Chief Waller said, "Sidney, I've lived near you a long time, and I was a good friend to your father. Now I want you to tell me the true story about what happened."

Sidney looked up for the first time and quietly said, "Okay, I will."

Chief Waller relaxed and hoped the boy would finally come clean. "Who killed your father?"

Without remorse or emotion, Sidney told the story.

I did it myself. We had words. Father came home, and we talked for a while. Then he commenced to criticize me; said I was uneducated and unfit to do for myself and make a living. He said it was my mother's fault. And then he commenced to abuse her and said she was not respectable and cursed her. That angered me, for I have a violent temper. I went out to the neighbor's woodshed and got the axe. When I came back, I kept it behind my back. Father started the same talk again, and I killed him. Then I dragged the body downstairs, put it in a wheelbarrow and dumped it in the alley.

Crime CRIM INSANE Term Indeterm
County Spokane Age 39-28
Rec'd 12-27-06 H'ght 6' 3½"
M. Exp. Eyes Blue
Nat'vty Washington Hair Dk-Br-Bld
Occup. None Blood
Record
Transferred to Medical Lake
Hospital 7-1-13.
Released Ret'd from Medical Lake
Hospital 6-6-28
1-16-29-released in custody on
court order Spokane county.
over

W.S.P.
4351

Teenager Sidney Sloane hacked his father to death with an axe in 1906. He was considered insane and released from Walla Walla prison on January 16, 1929. *Courtesy of Washington State Archives, Walla Walla Penitentiary records.*

Mr. Sloane was lying on a slab at the Buchanan Undertaking Company when Sidney was officially arrested for his murder. Since Sidney was not eighteen years of age, he would not be tried as an adult.

Dr. A.E. Pope's autopsy revealed "six wounds to the back of the head and on the face. The former cut through the scalp and fractured the bones of the skull. Food was found in the victim's mouth. The wounds that caused the death were one and a quarter inches long and three quarters of an inch wide, evidently made by a sharp instrument. The blows were delivered from behind the victim and while the head was bent forward."

Apparently, Sloane was eating dinner when Sidney decided to kill him. Spokane coroner Dr. F.P. Witter also disclosed his findings:

> *We found there was partially masticated food, bread and milk, in the mouth and that the man's stomach contained food that had barely been swallowed when the blows were struck. The man was unquestionably in the act of eating when he was slain. The position of the blows of the axe indicates that the gashes that cut through the man's skull were on the back of the head, indicating that he was bending over the table when the weapon fell. There was no struggle. The skull was badly fractured on each side, and the blows were so severe that they had cracked it lengthwise from the forehead to the base.*

During the trial, Mrs. Lily Syphers (a boarder in the Sloane home who was upstairs in her room at the time of the murder) was brought to the witness stand. She told the courtroom her version of what she witnessed:

> *On the night of the homicide, I was awakened, at what hour I cannot say exactly, by a noise of someone running in a light pair of shoes, running rapidly across the floor of the room occupied by the Sloanes. My mother's and my room is directly above it. Following this rushing noise came a sound of a heavy body falling. I fell back asleep and did not wake until the next morning about 5:30 a.m., when I was roused by the sound of someone using a hose outside my window.*

Why did Lily not wake up her mom or go investigate the strange sounds? This question was never asked.

The bookkeeper for the Sloane-Paine Company during the time of the homicide, Herman Smith, was brought to the stand. He told the court:

> *In my briefings with Mr. Sloane, I found he would often speak gibberish, he was confused, he would ask me to dictate absolute nonsense, he would call me by the wrong name, he would overdraw the accounts and was generally drunk most of the time. I thought Sidney was for sure insane. He would tell me wild stories: that he was engaged to thirty-two different ladies, of his bizarre money-making schemes and that he was going to raise expensive goats in Wyoming. One time he went into a craze and broke into the wine cellar, busted the top off a bottle of wine and proceeded to drink it straight from the broken bottle.*

Vera Luderman testified that one night at the theater, Sidney had suffered from one of his "fits." (It was disclosed after the trial that Vera and her father had practiced her false claim for over a month before being put on the stand.)

More witnesses spoke of Sidney's strange actions, from stealing items from the office to becoming wildly enraged during an innocent game of pool. One of the most damaging allegations against Sidney came from the family's former cook, a Chinese man named H.D. Lee. He took to the stand and told a very disturbing story about Sidney: "One time, Sidney got an axe and chased his smaller brother around the house, talking and screaming irrationally."

Deputy Prosecuting Attorney Fred Pugh told the jury their options for sentencing: "If he is convicted of murder in the first degree, he will be hanged. Murder in the second degree will be ten years to life in prison. Manslaughter would get him a sentence of one to twenty years." He wanted to make sure the jurors knew the consequences of their sentence for Sidney before they came to their decision.

While Sidney was being held, R.A. Mitchell was his cell mate. Sidney told Mitchell, "I will go to the insane asylum at Medical Lake until I am 21, and then go free. All the talk about me being crazy is a lie. It is hard for me to sit there and hear lies being told about me, but all this is being done to save my neck so I will have to stand for it."

The lengthy trial lasted for forty-two days. Attorney Robertson finally announced, "Sidney Sloane is found *not guilty* of the murder of Mr. James Sloane due to temporary insanity. Both his mother and myself agree that he shall be kept in custody until his sanity is proven, locked up for life if necessary."

As Sidney was being led from the courtroom back to the jail, he sneered at Sheriff Doak and said, "Well, we stuck it into you, didn't we?" and laughed.

Sheriff Doak was not amused and replied, "Shut up, you little whelp."

The next item the court would have to agree on was whether Sidney was to be sent to the state penitentiary or an insane asylum. It was decided Sidney would go to the Walla Walla State Penitentiary. The boy dressed in a fine black suit (the same suit that was the very reason the boy lost his temper the night of the killing). Sidney had desired a new suit and went to the tailor the very day before he butchered his dad. The tailor needed a twenty-five-dollar deposit in order to sew the custom suit. That evening, Sidney asked his father for the money, but he refused. Sidney lost his temper and grabbed the axe. Ironically, for the trial, his mother paid the tailor the money required to make the suit so Sidney would have a nice one to wear.

Now, as Sidney rode the train, with Sheriff Doak sitting by his side, he was again wearing the very same suit. When they stopped at a diner on the way to the prison, Sidney had a ferocious appetite and ordered oysters as well as just about everything else on the menu. Doak only picked at his food. He was disgusted by Sidney.

Sidney Sloane became inmate #4351 at the Walla Walla State Penitentiary on December 27, 1906. He was then eighteen years old and listed as "criminally insane." Attorney Roberts announced, "I will not be doing habeas corpus proceedings to try to free Sidney. I do not want him freed and he is to be treated as an insane person, not a criminal."

Records indicate that Attorney Robertson and Ida Huff, Sidney's mother, were trying to get Sidney released just a few years later. He was finally released from Walla Walla on January 16, 1929.

Sidney later got married, at age sixty, to Ruth King, and they lived a quiet life as farmers in the Nine Mile area in Spokane. When Sidney was seventy-eight, he was admitted to St. Luke's Hospital in Spokane, where, after thirteen long days, he eventually succumbed to acute congestive heart failure and died. No autopsy was performed.

Grandmother Murders Her Illegitimate Grandchild by Strangulation

Mrs. Jeannette Harris looked like any other grandmother: a little plump, soft spoken and plainly dressed. But lurking underneath her thick skirts and long, dark hair was a cold-blooded killer.

It all started on the Northern Pacific train she was riding from Yakima, Washington, to Spokane on June 11, 1903. She departed the train with a baby wrapped in her arms. The Black porter noticed the women seemed extremely agitated and distraught and in no shape to care for a baby. Concerned, he notified the police. Officer Tom Smith was called out to question the woman, but she could not be located.

Suspicions ran deeper as Harris returned to the train later that night—without the baby. When questioned, Harris simply stated, "I left it with friends."

But the employees of the Northern Pacific sincerely had their doubts and felt something was not right. When the police tried to locate Harris, they eventually found her hiding in the women's toilets. She was taken to the police station for questioning.

There, Captain McPhee began interrogating the woman, but she stuck to her story about leaving the baby with friends. McPhee wasn't buying it. She was locked up for the night in the city jail.

Around midnight, Detectives Briley and Logan took a shot at breaking down the woman's story. She was led back into the interrogation room. Now tired, weak and almost hysterical with fear, Harris began to crumble. By 1:00 a.m., Harris was ready to tell the truth: "I let the infant fall accidentally, and its head struck on a rock, crushing its skull. I was frightened by the accident and left the tiny corpse where it had fallen. We came to Spokane to give it up for adoption."

The detectives and McPhee knew in their hearts that they had a murder on their hands.

Harris said she would lead the detectives to the baby's dead body first thing in the morning. It would be a long night.

As soon as the sun began to rise, the detectives woke Harris, and they began their trek. The men and Harris began walking together down Stevens Street, then along Sprague Avenue to Division Street, until they headed south. They slowly traveled through gardens and brush, through small creeks and hills. At Fifth Avenue, they crossed through Crowley Springs and walked to the edge of a bluff, along a ravine and then one hundred feet up a hill. That was where Harris stopped, her feet firmly planted, and pointed down into a ravine. The horrifying sight of a dead baby loomed below.

Detective Briley turned to Harris angrily and said, "Now we want you to tell us, Mrs. Harris, just how you killed it!"

The old woman fell to her knees.

Briley repeated his question a few more times. Finally, Harris rose from the dewy ground and straightened her skirts, recomposing herself. "I choked it," she said coldly.

"How did you choke it? You need to tell us how you did it," Briley demanded.

"I tied a string around its neck and threw it into the bushes and left the string tied."

After her confession, there was nothing but silence.

Finally, Detective Logan shook off his shock and began making his way down into the ravine where the tiny corpse was wrapped in a small blanket. The poor babe was a purple hue due to the deliberate strangulation. Officer Logan noticed the cord had been wrapped deliberately around the infant's neck multiple times, removing all doubt that the murder was an accident.

Slowly, the police and Harris made the long trek back to the city jail in silence. Harris was promptly put back behind bars.

A trial for Harris began at 10:55 a.m. on September 21, 1904, with a jury of twelve men. During the trial, Harris remained unemotional, while her daughter, Pearl, was hysterical and cried constantly when the manner by which the baby died was presented. Many felt it was all for show.

Witnesses began disclosing very bizarre and telling evidence against the Harris family. The porter on the Northern Pacific train, J.L. Franklin, disclosed that he had seen Harris on the train with the baby. He heard it cry several times, so the baby was obviously alive at the time of their travels.

Thomas Smith, the night officer at the depot, told the jury that at 10:00 p.m., he saw Harris alone in the depot's waiting room, looking very nervous, sitting in a rocking chair. He noted she had a very worried look on her face, was wearing a wig and a shawl over her shoulders and appeared to be trembling. She held no baby. Smith called the police, concerned about the woman.

Officer Fitzharris arrived and asked Harris where the baby was. "On the hill," she responded. "Where on the hill?" he asked her. "I don't know. I have forgotten the name of the house." She then went into the ladies' toilet room and locked the door. Fitzharris beat on the door, demanding she come out immediately. She ignored his knocks and demands. Captain McPhee had arrived by then. "Where is the baby, Mrs. Harris?" he asked.

"The baby is dead. I lied to you at the station."

He promptly arrested Harris when she finally exited the ladies' room. The shawl had been left in the ladies' room and was gathered as evidence.

Coroner Smith was called to the witness stand and testified, "The baby was born healthy and all of its organs were normal.

Dr. H.R. Wells was next to testify. He said that no one even knew that Pearl was pregnant. Just a few days before she delivered, she had gone out dancing all night. Pearl had never even had to wear maternity clothes. When he arrived at the bedroom, Pearl was already in labor. He asked Mrs. Harris to boil water and get linens, but she ignored him and instead went to her daughter's side, muttering to her, "My God, Pearl, why have you done this?!"

After the baby was delivered, Mrs. Harris placed it at the foot of the bed. He advised her to clean and dress the child, but those suggestions were also ignored. She seemed extremely confused.

"What can be done to the man who ruined my daughter?" she simply asked the doctor. She then suggested that maybe someone could care for the baby for six months until they could go and retrieve it and raise it. It was disclosed that Harris had lost a baby fifteen years earlier and had suffered from emotional trauma ever since. Dr. Wells just thought the woman was insane.

Mrs. Shaw, from the Home of the Friendless shelter in Spokane, was brought to the stand. She stated, "Mrs. Harris came to our door with the baby. We had to refuse the child because it was from another county, not Spokane. The baby looked blue from exposure to the cold. I gave her my shawl to wrap the baby up in it. She asked me to care for the baby for a few months until she could retrieve it. We could not."

Next, Nellie Thornton was brought out as a witness. Nellie had been a cellmate of Harris's when she was in prison, and the woman had confessed to her what had happened the night the baby was born. Thornton testified:

> *Mrs. Harris said that her daughter had no love for the child and that on the night it was born she told her mom that if she didn't kill it, she would. So the next morning she boarded the train to Spokane. They had tried to smother it the night before by wrapping it tightly in a blanket, but the doctor had caught them. She thought she should have pierced the child's head with a hat pin, then the trip to Spokane would have never taken place.*

Harris was convicted of murder in the first degree and scheduled for the scaffold in Spokane County for murdering her illegitimate grandchild. No further records can be found of the final outcome of her fate.

The baby never even had a name.

Chapter 4

GAMBLING, DRUGS AND CRIME IN SPOKANE

I can say there will be no open gambling. If there is, arrests will be made!
—Spokane chief of police Leroy Waller, 1904

Spokane had a penchant for illegal activities, thus procuring the livelihoods of thugs, prostitutes, thieves, gamblers, drunks and everyone in between who wanted to invite trouble. By 1891, the population in Spokane had reached somewhere between twenty-five thousand and twenty-eight thousand citizens. The underworld of crime skyrocketed, keeping the police very busy. The officers were determined to shut down the illegal gambling halls, opium dens and houses of ill fame. Most arrests were under the charges of disorderly conduct, public drunkenness and vagrancy—violation of the city's ordinances.

The county jail was filling up fast. In 1910, the police department disclosed its numbers. In one year, the department had arrested 5,144 people, and its patrol wagon had traveled 1,864 miles.

The death penalty went into effect as part of Washington's Territorial Law in 1854 and continued until 1913, when it was abolished. The death penalty returned to Washington in 1981. Four hangings became part of Spokane's history. The first to swing from the gallows was Charles Brooks, a Black man who shot and killed his wife in 1891. The second was a Chinese man named Gin Pong in 1897, who butchered Lee Tung with two axes—one in each hand. The third hanging was that of George Webster, who killed his boss's wife in 1897. The fourth death to be scheduled was for a man named H.D. Smith, who killed a farmer named John Wyant in 1892.

The employees at the Spokane Courthouse were kept very busy between the gamblers, boozers, prostitutes and criminals who roamed the city. *Courtesy of Ian Sane, creativecommons via Wikimedia Commons.*

Smith was in jail waiting on his appeal. But on July 18, 1895, when the jailor brought the men their lunch, the forgetful officer forgot to lock the door behind him. The prisoners took advantage of his mistake and soon tried to flee the prison. Smith actually managed to break away and run for his life. Two officers quickly ran after him, and another jumped on a bicycle to try to capture Smith. Smith, frantic to get away, jumped into the icy, raging waters of the Spokane River. The current became too hard for him, and exhaustion soon plagued the prisoner. Nearby fishermen heard the calls from the policemen ashore and realized that Smith was wanted. In order to try to help the officers, the fishermen grabbed Smith by his shirt collar and tried to pull him aboard their boat. But much to their horror, Smith held a razor and, without hesitation, slashed his own throat. Shocked, the fishermen let go of Smith, who quickly drowned and sank to the bottom of the river.

During the fiasco, another twenty prisoners also escaped the jail but were quickly captured.

CALAMITY JANE IN SPOKANE

Calamity Jane, one of America's most notorious Wild West women, graced the city of Spokane with her presence in the late 1880s. She loved to deal the card game called faro and was very good at it (when she wasn't drunk!). When the Northern Pacific Railroad was laying its tracks through Spokane, Jane was enticed by the bustle and money being claimed by mining in the Coeur d'Alene region. Those who were cashing in on the silver claims were eager to spend their fortunes, and Spokane beckoned for them to do it within its city limits.

She began dealing faro at a little wooden building that was located next to the Owl Bar & Café (situated on the corner of Main Avenue and Howard Street). Soon, her rowdy reputation and unusual appearance caused many men to play a game with this "woman dressed like a man." They found it amusing that she could out-cuss, out-drink and out-smoke any man. She dressed up in her signature buckskin outfit and rawhide boots, carried her pistols and wore her hair short. She was proud of the fact that she could smoke a cigar while chewing tobacco at the same time.

Locals didn't harass her because it was rumored that if you sassed Calamity Jane, she would just as soon shoot you as fight with you. They had heard that she had been involved in a duel with a man named "Squint" Squires, and now he had only one arm because she shot the other one off. They had also heard that this was her last husband and they had lived together near Deadwood, South Dakota. They had argued about who was going to run the household and decided to settle the argument over a duel. Jane was a very good shot…

Jane drank her whiskey neat and was always the first one up to the bar. She was known to help anyone in need or those who had become sick. Often, she was the only person who offered assistance. After Calamity's death in 1903, the citizens of Spokane spoke fondly of Jane and her time in their city.

Calamity Jane graced Spokane with her excellent faro-dealing skills in the late 1800s in a little shack next to the Owl Bar & Café (situated on the corner of Main Avenue and Howard Street). *Courtesy of C.E. Finn of Livingston, Montana, Library of Congress.*

ILLEGAL GAMBLING IN SPOKANE

Private games of poker were allowed, but open games were illegal and considered a felony. If found guilty, a player could serve up to one year in jail. At times, up to ten active poker games would be going at the same time in downtown Spokane. The illicit activity was often performed in the back of cigar stores and saloons—which were often frequented by lawyers and prominent men of the city. Passwords were used at the front door to ensure privacy and secrecy to the players involved. Sometimes a crude handmade sign was hung on the front doorknob reading, "Rubberneckers are not wanted here!"

Chips cost five cents for white and twenty-five cents for red. Sore losers (when finally awakened from their drunken stupor) would often pull the trick of threatening to go to the police and turn the establishment in if they didn't get their money returned to them.

The clever invention of marked cards became even more interesting as print shops had the technology to design decks with hidden codes on the

A typical barroom scene with unidentified men playing poker in 1913. *Courtesy of S.T. Melander, Library of Congress #2012646440.*

A group of unidentified men in a saloon gambling, playing cards and roulette in 1910. A local sheriff, *right*, leans against the bar. *Courtesy of Library of Congress #2012649628.*

backs of the cards. Thicker or darker lines, small cues, series of dots or patterns were all used so that the dealer would know who had what cards in their hands. Tricky!

Two raids were made in the fall of 1904, putting a few Spokane men behind bars. Arthur Rumpel, who owned the Lobby Saloon on the corner of Front Avenue and Howard Street, was tossed in the slammer, along with M. Anderson and J.H. Fraser, who ran a saloon on Stevens Street and were also caught conducting poker games.

One of the busiest hot spots for a game was the back of the Havana Cigar Shop on Sprague Avenue near the Peyton Building.

More eyebrows went up, and Spokane's prosecuting attorney, Horace Kimball, was furious when Spokane's mayor, Frank Boyd, walked into a hot stud poker game happening at the Combination Saloon on the corner of Main Avenue and Stevens Street, watched it for a while and made no arrests.

"I will prosecute these gamblers and send them all to the penitentiary if it is the last thing I ever do! It is the most damnable outrage I have ever heard of!" Kimball yelled to anyone who would listen. Boyd shrugged it off, claiming he knew it was just a setup for his competing Democratic Party to try to disgrace him and the Republican Party.

Soon, the officers were told they would no longer be allowed to enter any saloons between sundown and sunrise. Some speculated that this new rule was actually so the officers could not witness the illegal gambling.

Detective Miles was not so easily played. He raided a gambling den at 516 Front Avenue (just a half block from Spokane City Hall) and threw a handful of men to the slammer. During this time, Chief of Police Sullivan was determined to halt all gambling in the Chinese and Japanese communities. He was tired of their opium dens, too. In one day, he arrested fifty offenders.

But a year later, in 1910, an eyebrow was raised by many when Chief of Police Sullivan's brother, Denny Sullivan, was somehow always allowed to play illegal games at his cigar shop without the risk of arrests.

SPOKANE'S CRIME WAVE IN 1910

The year 1910 was a hard one for the Spokane Police Department because crime was becoming so rampant in the city that they could hardly keep up with it. In October alone, they had fourteen robberies in ten days. The citizens and business owners were getting fed up and were accusing the police of being lazy.

The list of recent crimes in Spokane included:

- two men were badly beaten up and robbed—no arrest made
- two Italian men were shot while resisting to be robbed—no arrest made
- one man was lured into a Great Northern freight shed, robbed and beaten and choked almost to death—no arrest made
- almost nightly, citizens' homes were robbed—no arrests made
- a tourist from Massachusetts was robbed while walking down Howard Street—no arrest made
- jewels and a seventy-five-year-old Swiss watch were stolen from H. Dean's home on Liberty Avenue—no arrest made
- tools were stolen at George Young's butcher shop on First Street—no arrest made
- when Andy Dalby fell asleep in a saloon on Stevens Street, he was robbed of the forty-two dollars he had in his pockets—no arrest made

Spokane police raiding a gambling den in a basement of the Quick Lunch building on Thirteenth Street in January 1925. Cohen & Huches, Inc. is on the left, along with Delco Light Company, and Charlie's Laundry is on the left. *Courtesy of Library of Congress #2016839227.*

- R. Sylvester was robbed of his watch while he was sleeping at the Rix Bar—no arrest made
- at the Home Telephone Company, $100 worth of supplies was stolen—no arrest made
- local George Duffy was robbed and beaten nearly to death while walking down Division Street—no arrest made

With all this crime, it was no wonder the police were being accused of not doing their job. It is interesting to learn how the police captured criminals and solved crimes in the old days, before the modern-day luxuries of forensics, DNA, fingerprints and databases. These brave and intelligent men often only had a tiny clue, such as a missing button, a partial footprint, gossip or hearsay (and hopefully confessions), to solve a crime. Unless a criminal was caught in the act, it was very hard to prove who had done what.

Construction of the grand Monroe Street Bridge with its dimensions of 780 feet long, 135 feet high (from water) and span of main arch at 281 feet. *Courtesy of Library of Congress #LC-USZ62-121882.*

Spokane's Skid Row

Almost every state has a section of a major city that is termed "Skid Row," and Spokane was no different. Its Skid Row was located, oddly, near the public safety building at Howard and Front. The immorality stretched all the way to Sprague and Riverside Avenues, where legitimate business owners frowned on its very existence. Bawdyhouses, opium dens and gambling halls were oozing corruption and sin. City ordinances did nothing to stop the vagrancy, and even fines as hefty as $100 barely slowed down these wicked people.

Prostitutes, drunks and gamblers had to show up on the first Monday morning of the month in front of a city official, plead guilty and pay their fine (usually just five dollars). These fines became an excellent source of regular income for the city. The police would then leave the vagrants alone for the next few weeks, until the first of the month rolled around again, and the process would repeat itself once again.

Gambling Leads to Another Murder

Although Chief of Police Peter Mertz tried his hardest to get Spokane under control, his efforts were in vain. He demanded all illegal gambling

stop immediately, and any saloons or halls that were allowing gambling were to be closed and fined. He was also trying to crack down on all the drug activity in Spokane; opium, cocaine and morphine were widely used. The city ordinances prohibiting vagrancy, public drunkenness and disorderly conduct were simply ignored by many people. Arrests were at an all-time high but did little to banish the bad behavior of these men and women.

Open gambling resumed in 1892, despite all the police force's labors. The citizens of Spokane were not going to comply with the rules.

Two drinking and gambling buddies, Billy Fay and Jack Delmore, were amusing themselves on June 29, 1892, by drinking around town and playing faro at the Owl Saloon. Around 7:00 p.m., the men were completely intoxicated and began fighting over money. They were pushed out into the street by the weary bartender.

As they walked along Main and Howard, their anger escalated until they both reached for their revolvers. Shots were fired back and forth between the two men. Fay's first bullet hit nothing, but his second bullet pierced Delmore's side and went right through him. Delmore fell to the ground, bleeding. Fay shot at him again, and this bullet hit his hand. Despite his injuries, Delmore shot back at Fay but missed. He was somehow able to get up and started running away from Fay. He fell in a bloody heap on the steps of the Old National Bank building.

Help was summoned, and Delmore was quickly ushered to the doctors at Sacred Heart Hospital. The physicians were unable to save him, as he had lost a lot of blood. He requested his shoes be removed and then said, "Tell my folks that I died happy and that this was all a mistake."

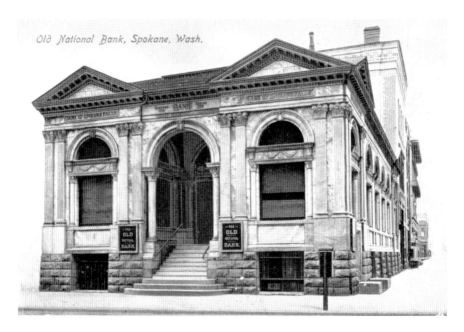

A postcard of the beautiful Old National Bank building (originally the Bank of Spokane Falls), where Jack Delmore died on the steps on June 29, 1982. *Courtesy of Spokane Public Library, Northwest Room.*

He died an hour after his arrival, and Fay was promptly arrested. Fay told the officers, "He threatened to kill me!"

Fay was charged with manslaughter, but in September, the jury considered his actions self-defense, and he was acquitted.

Two best friends torn apart over gambling and heavy drinking—exactly what Chief Mertz was trying to avoid for his city.

Spokane's Dirty Chinatown District

One of the most well-known old areas in town was Chinatown, also called Trent Alley. It was located approximately between Front Avenue (today Spokane Falls Boulevard) and Main Avenue, east from Howard Avenue on to Bernard Street—running about four blocks. This part of town was laced with opium dens, illegal gambling and houses of ill repute. A small section of Chinatown (now the Riverfront Park area) was completely eradicated by a fire in 1889.

The Chinese population in Spokane basically started around 1883 when the railroad came through. In 1882, the Chinese Exclusion Act denied citizenship to Chinese immigrants, and it was unlawful for their wives to come to the United States. This meant Chinatown consisted mostly of men. The famous Lotus Block section (also called Havana Block) of Chinatown kept Detectives Thompson and Miles very busy. In 1905, they arrested three Chinese men and one Black woman and confiscated seven opium pipes. A few months earlier, they had arrested two other Chinese men, Hop Sing and his friend Ah Yen, at their store on Front Avenue for pushing opium out of their backroom.

In 1907, the streets of Chinatown were bustling with activity. Honest businesses were run by Quong Ying Chun, Sing Fat & Company, Sun Lee Yick and Yee Yuen Hong Kee and Company. In 1910, approximately six hundred people were living in Chinatown. Some of the businesses in Trent Alley were the Square Deal Hotel, Eagle Hotel, North Western Hotel, Clem Hotel, Oregon Restaurant, Grand Café, Taximoto, Tokyo Dye Works, Seattle Café, Naxai Grocery and Panama Café. Along Bernard Street there was the Sunrise Café, Azuma-Toko and Saeki Dye Works.

The popular section of Chinatown soon exploded even more when the Japanese immigrants began moving there and more businesses began to open. Unfortunately, many young Japanese women were tricked into coming to the United States for work and ended up being sold to work in brothels.

But the fall of 1913 brought trouble to the Spokane neighborhood when several masked robbers broke into Sing Fat's store and ordered his wife, the terrified Sue Ah Yen, and their three kids into the backroom. The crooks

Five unidentified criminals lining up for a photograph at McNeil Island Penitentiary. *Courtesy of ancestry.com, McNeil Island Penitentiary records.*

Eight unidentified Chinese men gambling. Many of the old buildings in Chinatown were demolished to allow parking for the spectacular Spokane Expo in 1974. *Courtesy of Library of Congress #2001705605.*

proceeded to steal all of Sing Fat's jewelry and cash. They were never caught.

Around 1940, Chinatown began to fade away, and slowly, others moved into the buildings. Many of the old buildings of Chinatown were demolished to build up for the spectacular Spokane Expo in 1974. The last building was torn down to make way for the construction of the parking lot for the new convention center. Researchers unearthed many objects from old Chinatown that were lodged under the Looff Carrousel (also known as the Riverfront Park Carousel and the Natatorium Park Carousel). They found bits of porcelain plates and cups with symbols and writing on them.

The original carousel was built in 1909 by Charles I.D. Looff for his daughter Emma Vogel and her husband, Louis. It remained at Natatorium Park until 1968, when the park closed. The carousel was then moved in 1975 to Riverfront Park, where it still delights people today.

OPIUM, NOODLE JOINTS AND UNDERAGE BEER GUZZLING

The worst menace to the youth of this city is found in the noodle joints conducted by the Chinamen. If there is any way under the heavens by which I can close these noodle joints, I am going to do it!
—*Spokane chief of police Leroy Waller, 1904*

The Spokane police had their hands full when it came to controlling the Chinese crimes in Spokane. The Chinese community was tightknit, and they rarely went to the police for problems; instead, they chose to resort to taking care of matters themselves.

But the local noodle joints, as they were called, were creating a lot of problems for many normally upstanding citizens of the city. Teenagers and wives started hanging out in the dens. Some as young as twelve years old were caught guzzling beer and smoking. Respectable housewives were partaking in day drinking, too. Something had to be done.

Chief of Police Leroy Waller often raided these joints, hoping the fines and chaos would make the dens close down. The Chinese men were purchasing the beer, bringing it back to the den and then offering the beverage to local teenagers and women. Their motive was unclear and only speculative. One

Two of Spokane's Chinese immigrants, Jack Klane and Jim Williams, both in McNeil Island Penitentiary for second-degree murder. *Courtesy of ancestry.com, McNeil Island Penitentiary records.*

Opium dens were very popular in Spokane's Chinatown and kept the local police very busy. They were also known to supply beer to minors. *Courtesy of Library of Congress.*

of the boys caught guzzling booze was the son of a very wealthy, respectable and prominent Spokane businessman (name not disclosed).

Sergeant Sullivan and Officer Tom Lister were assigned to raid the noodle joints. Wa Tipp, proprietor of a noodle joint located at 612 Front Avenue, was raided and found to be selling beer to underage drinkers. He was fined $100 and had to sit in front of Judge Hinkle. The officers found two sixteen-year-old boys drinking there and two young girls ages twelve and fifteen swilling booze well after midnight. They were hauled off to the police station (along with the pitcher of booze as evidence), and their parents were called.

Sullivan and Lister decided to return to Tipp's den and see what else was going on there. Another group of young kids—four boys and three girls— had arrived and were engaging in drinking beer. Wa Tipp, with a sleepy opium-smoking look on his face, apparently did not learn his lesson.

Sergeant Sullivan told reporters the next day, "I have kept the names of these young people from the papers, but hereafter I shall stop the practice. Anyone from now on who is brought to the police station will be published! This will do more good in keeping down the crime than a term in jail. The parents of these young folks are prominent people!"

Sullivan's threat did not seem to deter the noodle joints from selling booze to minors nor stop the kids from drinking it there. For many years after his played-out threat of public exposure, the names of the boozers were published for all to see, but it did little to stop the underage drinking.

A Hidden Pouch Full of Jewels

A series of serious burglaries was making Spokane residents and tourists very nervous. No one was safe from being robbed, and the police had been unable to catch the thief or thieves. Most of the crimes were committed against wealthy tourists staying at the Pennington Hotel and nearby housing. People were getting frustrated with the police department and started accusing them of not doing their job.

In July 1909, Mr. and Mrs. Hunt were visiting Spokane and were taking their stay at the Pennington Hotel. They soon became victims. Their precious jewels were stolen from their rooms practically right before their eyes. Mrs. DeLion was also a victim of robbery, having $650 worth of diamonds stolen from her.

The Second Monroe Street Bridge replaced the rickety wooden one that burned down in 1890. *Courtesy of Spokane Public Library, Northwest Room.*

As the police were trying to stop the thieves, a local laborer named John Heron became the hero. As he was walking along the river underneath the Washington Street Bridge viaduct, he noticed a sack tucked under a rock. It looked like an ordinary tobacco pouch. Bored and curious, he pulled the pouch from the rubble. Much to his surprise, when he opened it up, it was full of gold and jewels!

The honest Heron quickly took the loot to Officer DeLaney, who was on duty at the station. When DeLaney peered into the pouch, he, too, was amazed at its contents and Heron's honesty. Inside the grubby sack was Mrs. DeLion's stolen diamonds, four loose diamonds, two large rubies, two strands of pearls, a gold locket, a gold piece, a topaz scarf pin, two gold cuff links, a man's gold watch and chain and three one-cent stamps!

Mr. and Mrs. Hunt could not be located to return their stolen jewels, and whatever happened to them is a mystery. It is not known whether Heron received any type of reward for his honesty.

Spokane Killer Escapes Utah Penitentiary with Bullet in His Arm

While living in Spokane, James Lynch was known as a polite, hardworking and upstanding citizen. He was employed at the Turkish Bathhouse on Howard Street near Front Avenue as a "rubber." Towering over six feet tall, it was hard to miss him. How Lynch went from Spokane resident to prison escapee remains a mystery.

Somewhere along the line, Lynch and Robert King decided to hold up the famous Sheep Ranch gambling den in Salt Lake City, Utah. There, Lynch murdered Colonel Godfrey Prowse and was soon wanted by the authorities. After his capture, Lynch and King were scheduled to be executed a few weeks later.

A few days before his hanging, an angry mob of inmates somehow managed to plan and execute a break from the Utah State Penitentiary. With a couple of ladders, the inmates were determined to get over the wall and to freedom. But as they were climbing the ladders, the guards began firing at them.

After his capture, Lynch told his story to the *Salt Lake Herald*:

> *I was shot while going up the ladder. I did not know what was going on inside for I was in a big hurry to get away. I did not know of the* [prison] *break*

until I heard Waddell yell, "Get on yer clothes, you fellas!" and my cell door was opened and I ran out. When I got outside they were coming with the ladders and I was the first one up. As I got almost to the top the guard, Frank Naylor I believe, plunked away at me and got me here in the arm. The shock almost knocked me off the wall but I managed to get on top and fell over onto the outside. I hit the wall while falling and struck my back. I jumped up and ran for the creek, but I was blinded from the shot and the fall from the wall and I ran to the creek and when I was going to the other side of the bushes, I fainted. I came to after a while, but was so weak from the loss of blood that I couldn't get up at first. After fixing up my arm a little I finally got on my feet and kept on up the creek for a ways then cut over into the brush. I was awful weak and every once in a while would faint and keel over in some brush and at last I fell over into some brush and couldn't get up, so laid there until morning. It wasn't so bad that night but the next day my arm got pretty sore and I was still sore all over. The next night it rained. I traveled as well as I could by stopping and resting now and then, but it was slow work. I got wet and cold and was awful hungry. After that I don't remember much. I kept on going and didn't meet anybody and finally got out there [Wood's Cross]. I knew I was taking a big risk by going into town but I had to have something to eat. I felt sure I was going to die, anyhow, so didn't care much what happened. I got some bread and meat at a farm house and then these fellas came along and picked me up.

Spokane resident James Lynch murdered Colonel Godfrey Prowse at the famous Sheep Ranch gambling den in Salt Lake City, Utah. *Drawing courtesy of author, original photograph from the* Salt Lake Herald, *October 15, 1903.*

After Lynch escaped prison, he tried to find refuge in a neighboring barn. At John Hill's place one morning, Hill's eight-year-old daughter was sent out to the barn to fetch an item. When she returned, she told her parents, "I saw some blankets move."

They ignored the young girl's comment, believing she was imagining things.

Yet when Mr. Hill went to the barn later, as he climbed the ladder to reach the hay loft, he spotted blood. There was also blood all over a pile of hay. He also noticed his rubber raincoat was missing from the barn. Hill notified the police.

Soon, Lynch was found and captured near Wood's Cross by brothers Gilbert and Philando Hatch, who were eager for the $500 reward.

Lynch was exhausted and weak both from blood loss and lack of food and water; he hadn't eaten in five days. His left arm had been severely damaged by the guard's bullet, and blood poisoning had set in, leaving his arm black all the way up to his shoulder.

"I am glad it is all over, but I wish I could've gotten away," was all he said to the police when they arrived.

As he was unloaded back at the Utah prison, Lynch was so weak the men had to practically carry him into his old cell. The prison physician, A.C. Young, was called and examined Lynch. The main part of his forearm had been shot away, but the doctor felt his arm could be saved.

King decided to become an avid student of Shakespeare until his sentence was finished, and Lynch decided to learn to play the guitar.

THE MOST BRUTAL OF HOLDUPS

In March 1906, Spokane fireman W.D. Riley was walking home after his shift. It was around 7:45 p.m. when he was heading down Carlisle Avenue toward his house on Division Street. He noticed two strangers approaching him, so he quickened his pace. Then he began running toward his house just twenty feet away. He arrived safely, but the door was locked. He tried desperately to get it open, to no avail. He headed to the back door, hoping it would be unlocked and he could get away from the thugs.

Unfortunately, the men pounced on Riley and savagely beat him over the head with a wooden club. They stole his watch and checked his pockets for money, of which he had none. They took off running, leaving poor Riley in a pool of blood. He tried to crawl to his house to bang on the windows to get the attention of someone inside, but he was too weak. Just then, the milk boy was coming back from his porch, where he had just left a jug of fresh milk for the Riley family.

Riley, fearing for the boy's life too, yelled, "Run for your life!" The boy, seeing Riley's smashed face, took off running. A long thirty minutes later, his mom finally opened the back door to retrieve the milk the boy had left. She heard her son's groans and ran to his side. She helped him into her house and quickly summoned a doctor. Riley's nose had been bashed into his face, making it almost impossible to breathe. The doctor worked on Riley for over two hours trying to save his life. Fortunately, he was successful, and Riley survived his assault.

Just two hours later, the thugs were at it again. This time, their victim was a man named Samuel Arnold, who lived on Sprague Avenue. The strangers hit him over the head with their club, too, hoping to rob him of any valuables. They left him for dead lying in the street in a pool of his own blood. All they got was another watch. Officer Hook was on patrol nearby, and when he saw the men attacking Arnold, he came running. The men took off. Hook yelled, "Halt!" but—imagine this—the thieves kept running. Hook pulled his gun and started shooting at the men but failed to hit any of them.

The three thieves refused to quit. Later that night, they approached a wagon driver named Ed McNeil. Two came up on his right and one on his left when he stopped his load on the east end of Sprague Avenue.

"Give us all your money!" they demanded of McNeil. The frightened McNeil did not know what to do. Luckily, a couple of other men came along, and the thieves ran off before attacking McNeil.

The robbers were never caught.

DID FAMOUS OUTLAW BUTCH CASSIDY ACTUALLY DIE IN SPOKANE?

Robert Leroy Parker died in the Northwest in the fall of 1937. Where he is buried and under what name is still our secret. All his life he was chased. Now he has a chance to rest in peace and that's the way it must be.
—*Lula Betenson, Butch Cassidy's youngest sister*

Legendary bank and train robber Butch Cassidy (1866–1908 or 1937? it is a mystery); real name: Robert LeRoy Parker; aliases: Jim Lowe, George Parker, Jim Maxwell, Jim Ryan, George Cassidy and Lowe Maxwell) was rumored to have escaped the supposed fatal shootout in Bolivia in 1908 and fled to Spokane, Washington, to live out his days in peace.

Many controversies and conspiracies surround Cassidy's death. The truth may never be discovered, and the mystery remains unsolved to many researchers and historians.

Butch Cassidy led a gang called the Wild Bunch (a group of ten outlaws) and partnered with the famous cowboy Harold Alonzo "Sundance Kid" Longbaugh in the early 1900s. They focused on bank and train robberies, a few of which made them very rich. But Cassidy was a good-hearted and kind criminal who made certain no civilians ever got hurt in their robberies.

Rumors suggest famous outlaw Butch Cassidy was never killed in Bolivia; instead, he had plastic surgery in Paris and then moved to Spokane to live out his life in peace. *Courtesy of the Wyoming Territorial Prison in Laramie, Wyoming, from 1894.*

It was even told how Cassidy helped a merchant with his overdue mortgage payment of $1,000.

Although the gang had "Wanted Dead or Alive" posters plastered all over the country for them (with a reward of up to $30,000), Cassidy was never arrested for robbery. In fact, the only time he was arrested was in 1894 for stealing a $5 horse.

The Wild Bunch robberies included;

- The crew's first robbery was committed on August 13, 1896, from a bank in Idaho when they stole $7,165.
- The gang robbed a train on April 21, 1897, and made out with $8,800.
- On June 2, 1899, they robbed a train in Wyoming and grabbed $60,000.
- In late June 1899, they robbed the San Miguel Valley Bank and made off with $20,750.
- On July 11, 1899, they got lucky and robbed a New Mexico train of a whopping $70,000.
- On August 29, 1900, they robbed another Wyoming train and took $55,000.
- On September 9, 1900, the bunch stole $32,640.

- On July 3, 1901, they made their last robbery in Montana for $65,000 and decided it was time to get out of America, as Pinkerton detectives were closing in on them. The gang split up, all going their own ways except for Cassidy and Sundance. They decided to go to Argentina. In today's currency, the gang stole over $10 million in their short careers as criminals.

Butch Cassidy, the Sundance Kid and Kid's girlfriend, Etta Place, fled to Argentina in 1901 for safety. The trio boarded the ship *Herminius* heading for Buenos Aires on February 20, with Cassidy posing as Etta's brother and renaming himself James Ryan.

For several years, they lived peacefully in a small four-room log cabin on fifteen thousand acres together in Cholila Valley. There, Etta hoped they could live a peaceful life away from the troubles of the law.

In June 1905, Sundance and Cassidy visited his brother Elwood Cassidy in San Francisco, California, before returning to South America. Unfortunately, the men soon got itchy fingers and began robbing banks again. On December 19, 1904, the gang robbed the Ban Coclé de la Nacion in Villa Mercedes and then fled to Chile.

A year later, Etta had become frustrated with the life of an outlaw. She wished to return to the United States. She regretted leaving their farm life behind. She probably regretted abandoning her simple life as a teacher, wife and mother to her two children to be with Sundance.

On June 30, 1906, Sundance accompanied her back to San Francisco, and the two never reunited again. Sundance returned to South America, and Etta simply disappears from history. (Note: On July 31, 1909, a woman who matched Etta's description tried to secure a death certificate for Sundance in order to "settle his estate.")

But on November 6, 1908, Cassidy and Sundance's luck ran out as they were tracked down in a small Bolivian village called San Vicente. The Bolivian police ambushed a group of criminals, and dozens of shots were fired. Two men, believed to be Cassidy and Sundance, were shot down dead by police. Some historians believe that the pair committed a murder/suicide where Cassidy shot his best friend Sundance in the head and then turned the gun on himself—a pact they had made to never go back to jail.

A friend of the dead men, Percy Seibert, voluntarily identified the two deceased as the much-wanted criminals. The men were buried sided by side in a small cemetery. No photographs of the dead men were ever taken. What the police did not know at the time was that Seibert knew the men were *not* Cassidy and Sundance. Seibert and his family had been helped by Cassidy many times while living in Bolivia and even said that he had saved their lives. Falsely identifying the men was his payback to them and a way for them to escape once and for all from the police.

So did Cassidy and Sundance really escape?

The conspiracy was that Cassidy had ventured off to Paris, France, to receive plastic surgery so he would no longer be recognized. Just two years after Cassidy and Sundance were "killed," a man named William Thadeus Phillips showed up in Spokane, Washington, and started a machine shop. He wrote a memoir near the end of his life titled *Bandit Invincible*, in which he told of Cassidy's travels and adventures, exposing little-known facts about Cassidy that some thought were indisputable proof that William Phillips was actually Butch Cassidy.

Some believe that Phillips's memoir was actually stories told by Cassidy to his fellow jail mate at the Wyoming Territorial Prison during the just under two years he served there. The jail mate was none other than William Phillips. Phillips was also known as Wilcox. Cassidy was released in 1896, and Phillips was released in 1908. The two apparently had robbed a few places together, served later together in jail and remained friends. When Phillips/Wilcox was released, he married Gertrude Livesay from Michigan and changed his name to Phillips. The pair moved to Spokane to start their life together.

To promote the Phillips/Cassidy theory further, Phillips owned a six-shot Colt revolver, just like Cassidy had, even including the same unique pistol grip. Handwriting analysis of the manuscript proved it was possible that the manuscript could have been written by Cassidy himself.

In 1991, forensic historians Dan Buck and his wife, Anne Meadows, gained access to the two graves of the bank robbers to hopefully secure DNA evidence proving once and for all whether the bones were those of Butch Cassidy and the Sundance Kid. But when the DNA tests were completed, the results were surprising.

The DNA for Sundance came back as "similar," and the DNA for Cassidy's "body" came back as of European descent. (Cassidy's DNA sample had been compared to his brother's DNA in Pennsylvania.)

The story gets even more complicated and confusing when Cassidy's younger sister, Mrs. Lula Parker Betenson, wrote her novel *Butch Cassidy, My Brother* in 1975. She claimed Cassidy came and ate blueberry pie with her in Circleville, Utah, in 1925. She claims he died from pneumonia near Spokane in 1937. A William Phillips did die on July 20, 1937, in Spangle, near Spokane. His body was cremated and his ashes scattered.

Lula tells that her brother's body was secretly buried near the log cabin he loved so much on the Parker family ranch. "Tom's old cabin" was a favorite place for Cassidy to go camping with his buddies. A neighbor, Marilyn Grace, revealed that on July 20, 1937, the family held some sort of secret "funeral" at the cabin.

Later, cadaver dogs searched the site and found a human spine bone and one toe bone. Could these be the remains of Butch Cassidy? Unfortunately, there was not enough DNA evidence to produce a positive identification. Lula stated that the family moved his body again to a new secret spot once they realized his final resting place had been discovered.

Who is telling the truth?

Did Cassidy really have plastic surgery in Paris to hide his identity in order to start a new life in Spokane, Washington? Was Phillips/Wilcox actually Cassidy? Was Cassidy really buried in an unmarked and hidden grave somewhere in Utah?

The world will never really know the truth about Butch Cassidy's final resting place. Or the Sundance Kid's, for that matter!

But a good mystery will always be more interesting than the truth.

Train Robbers and a Fight Over the Reward

In the fall of 1907, two train robbers were captured in Spokane and were held in the city jail by Chief of Police Rice. The men, C. McDonald and Ed Smith, had stolen $14,395 from a Great Northern train in Montana. Rice was frustrated and told reporters, "There is no way to hold them here because the train robbery occurred in Rondo, Montana. Neither is there any reason to hold them here because the Old National Bank was already reimbursed by the insurance company." The crooks were captured by Jesse Howe and Tom Riley, who were demanding McDonald and Smith be locked up until they received their reward money.

In an interesting twist, the robbers were captured the first time by Spokane detectives Lurns and Briley. Even though the robbers were locked up, the next morning, the detectives discovered that they had somehow managed to escape the city jail. Both McDonald and Smith *and* the $14,395 were gone!

Since the robbery occurred in Rondo but the thieves were captured in Spokane, a fight over the reward money ensued. The ridiculous list of people who were fighting over the reward money included Detectives Ryan

No. 1284	Name	McDONALD, Charles
Alias		
Crime	Burglary	
Age 21	Height 6'¼"	Weight
Build	Hair Dk Brn	Eyes Hazel
Comp.	Born	Oregon
Occupation Farmer		Nativity Am'r.
Rec'd from	Whitman Co. 7,27,94.	Sentence 3 yrs

Top: In 1907, train robbers Charles McDonald and Ed Smith were captured in Spokane and held in the city jail by Chief of Police Rice. They had stolen $14,395 from a Great Northern train. *Courtesy of Spokane Public Library, Northwest Room.*

Bottom: Train robber Charles McDonald was sentenced to prison for three years in 1894. *Courtesy of Washington State Archives.*

and Enright of the Great Northern Railroad; Sergeant McPhee of Spokane; Detectives McDonald and Briley of Spokane; Jesse Howe, a Spokane stable man; Tom Riley, a bartender in Spokane; attorney S.E. Henry; Mr. Cummings, proprietor of the Casey Hotel; and H.B. Walton, a train agent from Bonners Ferry, Idaho.

Walton felt he deserved the reward because he told Howe to follow the robbers and then notified the Spokane Police Department which train they were traveling on. Riley claimed that he was the one who telegraphed the police. The lawyer claimed he deserved the reward because Riley would not have told the police if he was not forced to do so by Henry.

Proprietors in Bonners Ferry told the police that the men were spending money like there was no tomorrow while visiting a dance hall there. They purchased very expensive kimonos for the prostitutes to wear and seemed to have no care as to what things cost.

No records can be found as to who exactly ended up with the reward or where the $14,395 ended up.

A Wife, a Fight and a Chewed-Off Finger

A jealous soon-to-be ex-husband named E.P. Fulton and his good buddy Charles Frozier were walking along Riverside Avenue in Spokane one night in March 1906. Ed Eusley was also walking down Riverside, accompanied by a lovely woman. When Fulton looked up, he noticed the beautiful lady was his wife!

"What are you doing with my wife?" Fulton yelled at Eusley.

"It's none of your business. She is not your wife but is a lady friend of mine. I will walk with her as much as I please."

This infuriated Fulton to no end, and he took a swing at Eusley. As the men continued to fight, Eusley unexpectedly took a big bite at his opponent's hand. His mighty jaws clamped down on Fulton's fingers, making the man scream as he pulled him over 150 feet from Riverside and along down Post Avenue. Frozier began choking Eusley, hoping this would make the man release his bite on the poor man's fingers. Finally, the bloody, mangled hand was released, and the police arrested Eusley on the charge of mayhem.

Doctors feared one of Fulton's fingers that was almost completely chewed off would have to be amputated. Luckily, the physicians were able to save the lovestruck man's finger.

Mrs. Fulton filed for a divorce.

Chapter 5

CONSPIRACY, CORRUPTION AND CRAZINESS

Spokane's Ruthless Bigamist

Some men cannot handle one wife, let alone multiple ones. But a society man from Spokane decided he would roll the dice on marrying several women in several different states. His strange marriage scandal left many hearts and homes broken.

Arlington Buckingham Wadsworth (what a spectacular name!) came to Spokane in 1902, portraying himself as a wealthy businessman. He appeared to be a charming, dashing and debonair gentleman; he was successful in real estate and rode gallant horses effortlessly. Men hated him, and women adored him. Everywhere he went in Spokane, he was surrounded by beautiful women, and he only hung around Spokane's elite crowd. He had his heart set on marrying Spokane's wealthiest single woman.

But Wadsworth was not who he pretended to be. Born in New York in 1847, his real name was Samuel Oakley Crawford. In 1864, he joined the army, and then in 1867, he became a Methodist preacher in New Jersey. He was a chameleon on many levels and was wanted by the police from Maine all the way to California. Wadsworth falsely posed as a lawyer, banker, politician, real estate developer, writer and mining speculator. He sometimes changed his name to Arthur Bentley Worthington…

In reality, he was a bigamist and con artist, with his marriage schemes starting when he was just seventeen years old.

His first wife was Josephine Ericson Moore. In 1868, after only a year of marriage, he deserted her and their one-year-old daughter to fend for themselves.

In 1870, he conned a farmer in Albany, New York, and stole a bunch of his money. He was arrested and sentenced to three years in jail.

As soon as he got out of jail, he fled to Washington and was back to his old tricks. In 1874, he married his second wife (not bothering to divorce his first one) in Spokane. She was the daughter of a wealthy clairvoyant in Boston. He deserted her too after just a year (also declining to divorce her).

His third wife was the daughter of a wealthy judge in Ohio. In 1875, Wadsworth greedily forged her name on a $3,000 bank note. When he knew he was caught, he fled to Kansas City, where he assumed the name Eugene Bonner.

The year 1876 found him in Peoria, Illinois. The police all over the country had had enough of his shenanigans, and reward posters began being plastered all over the place. This is where disgruntled wife #2 reappears. As soon as he knew she was on his tail, he fled to San Francisco to escape her wrath.

There, he married wife number four (although he was still not divorced from the other three), a wealthy and lonely widow. He nonchalantly stole $2,000 from her. He was not as clever as he thought though, and the police somehow got wind of his whereabouts. A telegram came through exposing him as a fraud and criminal. Again he was on the run and left San Francisco, heading for Salt Lake City, Utah. There he decided to become a Mormon. He told a sad tale to the local parishioners, and soon he was $5,000 richer.

He decided he better take the money and run, so he went to Texas next.

In 1878, he landed in Detroit, Michigan, and joined the circus. Well, what was one more wife at this point? He married wife number five, Miss Eliza Huntoon, and changed his name to Bannerton. They soon tired of the circus and moved to New Lisbon, Wisconsin, where he practiced law. His itchy fingers could not stop themselves, and he forged more bank notes and stole more money from locals. He was arrested but released on bail. He left wife number five and was on the move again.

During 1882, he traveled all over the United States in search of more opportunities.

In 1883, he pretended to be an English tourist in Boston. He practiced law and lived a very lavish lifestyle. To change things up a bit, this time he wooed a married woman to see if he could capture her love. Mrs. John Sargent fell head over heels for him and soon left her husband to become wife number six. They moved to Charleston, West Virginia, and lived happily ever after—until her money ran out.

In 1886, he swindled a married lady named Mrs. Dana out of $3,000.

He left town again and soon fell in love with another woman. They decided to run away to Chicago and get married (making her wife number seven). But right before the final hour, the bride-to-be's father was able to stop the ceremony.

Somewhere along the line, Wadsworth posed as a leader in a spiritual movement called Students of the Truth, where he conned and obtained money again under false pretenses.

Police everywhere were desperate to catch this bigamist and put an end to his ridiculous multi-marriages. Wadsworth was finally arrested in Melbourne, Australia, of all places in November 1902.

There would be no more marriages for him. It is not known if all his former wives eventually obtained divorces.

INTIMIDATION IN THE SPOKANE POLICE DEPARTMENT

Spokane's police force had its drama and troubles over the years, that's for sure. Sex with prisoners, sex with minors, bribes, payoffs…

Take the case of Colonel Tom Smith in 1904. Smith had aggressively assaulted Edward Meyers while in the Club Café Bar. Meyers had just popped in to see a man named Charley Tynan, the night bartender. Unfortunately, Meyers was too drunk to actually remember who it was that assaulted him.

Milo Waldron, another bartender, explained what happened. "Meyers came into the saloon. He spoke rudely to Smith. There proceeded with a slight scuffle. Smith then pushed him away. When Meyers came back at him, Smith struck him hard, but did not knock him down."

The other police officers were afraid to testify against Smith for fear of losing their jobs, for it was well known that Smith was protected by "Dutch Jake" Goertz, a local man to be feared, and his partner Harry Baer. Mayor Frank Boyd told the papers, "Goertz and Baer control most of the city officials."

But the mayor wished to file charges of criminal activity against Detective Martin Burns, knowing he was withholding evidence. He knew Burns had lied about something. Prosecuting attorney Kimbell tried his hardest, but the complaining party (Meyers) was "too drunk to remember the circumstances involved."

Regardless, Smith was tried and acquitted by Judge Hinkle on all charges filed against him. This infuriated the jurors, and they began burning office chairs in the judge's private chamber!

Burns was quietly suspended from the department for a few days for appearances. Detective Briley (who was also afraid of Burns) tried in vain to get any of the other policemen to gather evidence against Smith, but none would do it. They had mouths to feed.

The judge declared Smith not guilty.

Just goes to show it is sometimes not what you know, but who you know.

SPOKANE'S CAPTAIN COVERLY MARRIES THE WRONG GAL

The very handsome Spokane chief of police James Coverly found out the hard way that sometimes it is better to do your homework before marrying someone. He found himself in an awful mess.

When he married LuLu in Spokane on June 5, 1904, he did not know she was already married to another man named Billy Grossbeck. She had told him she was a widow. She also had a thirteen-year-old son. As soon as Coverly discovered LuLu had lied to him, he placed ads in the local papers and notified all the shop owners and bartenders not to allow LuLu to rack up any credit. It was embarrassing. But he had to do it.

LuLu knew the chief had three children with his first wife that he was trying to support. He had a son named Jesse and two daughters, Martha and Samantha. But LuLu didn't care.

Coverly was making the normal police officer's salary of $110 a month, plus $6 per month from his pension from the United States government. He paid $35 per month in child support, plus any of their medical bills. His son suffered from bad health, and his care alone cost $25 per month. Jesse got worse, and the hospital bill was racking up; it was almost $140. But LuLu did not care about that either. She demanded $100 from Coverly, or else. He had to borrow the $100 to shut her up. Now he was $240 in debt. LuLu continued to demand higher and higher sums for her clothing and luxuries or she was going to blackmail him. She had no problem lying to the public to dishonor him. All the while, LuLu refused to cook meals, clean the house or do laundry. She would verbally and physically abuse the poor man. She refused to let him sleep. She threatened to poison him if he didn't give her money. She even threatened to throw carbolic acid on his face to disfigure him for life. If that wasn't enough, she would go into his office and humiliate him in front of other people.

On December 19, 1904, Coverly had finally had enough of LuLu. He moved out of his house. He was hurt and confused. Before their marriage, she had conducted herself like a proper lady. In truth, she was a prostitute who lived with multiple men, a woman of the lowest character. When he found out, she yelled, "I never loved you, I only married you for the money! I will have your money at any cost and will resort to anything to force you to comply with my demands!"

LuLu continued to have affairs with other men, married or not.

Perhaps LuLu should have done her homework too and discovered Coverly lived on a meager wage and had another family to support.

Coverly was a handsome man and greatly respected in the police department and the community. He served the police department for twenty years. He happily lived out his life in Spokane until he died in 1920 at age seventy-one.

MUSICIAN PRETENDS TO BE A MAN UNTIL CORONER DISCOVERS TRUTH

In today's world, it seems utterly impossible that a person could not pursue their talents simply because they are a woman. But that was the sad truth for many women in history.

One of Spokane's most notorious and well-loved cross-dressers was a man/woman known as Billy Tipton, who entertained thousands of folks throughout his/her life all over the United States. But "Billy" was really "Dorothy."

Dorothy Lucille Tipton was born in 1914. Her life started out hard and became harder. After her parents divorced, she was shipped off to live with her aunt in Missouri. It was there she began her love affair with music, excelling in her talents. The problem was that she would not be allowed to join any bands or groups to play because she was a girl. Yet this would never deter Dorothy for as long as she lived.

She expertly learned to walk, dress, talk and assume the role of a man in order to promote her musical career around the 1930s. She wore her hair cut like a man and bound her breasts. She smoked cigarettes like a man. She even began living with women, whom she would introduce as "my wife." She changed her name to Billy Lee Tipton.

Her musical career blossomed, and she began touring gigs all over. She even began recording some albums. Assuming the role of a man became second nature to Billy, and even long after it became commonplace for women to work in the field, she never returned to being a female. Perhaps she didn't want the scandal, or perhaps she was just more comfortable living as a man.

Billy would go through a few more "wives," telling all of them that he was incapable of having sex due to a horrible auto accident that left him scarred and ultimately prone to erectile dysfunction. No one questioned Billy.

His career continued to grow, but although he got multiple offers to play all over the United States, he decided to make his beloved Spokane his permanent home. His band was called the Billy Tipton Trio, and they played at the Ridpath Hotel, the Davenport Hotel, the Green Monkey and the Tin Pan Alley regularly.

He married a fifth wife; they adopted three children and became a happy Spokane family.

After over forty years entertaining people as a jazz pianist disguised as a man, Dorothy/Billy succumbed to a bleeding ulcer on January 21, 1989. Billy was mourned by thousands of people.

But the world was shocked (along with his wife and kids) when the coroner disclosed that Billy was actually a woman.

It remains a mystery why Billy didn't go public with the fact that he was born a she. No one would have cared; in fact, they probably would have embraced her strength and determination to pursue her musical career when not allowed as a young girl.

The exposure of her true identity sparked shock, curiosity and debates. But one thing is certain: Billy/Dorothy was a wild and crazy person and a wonderful part of Spokane's outrageous and fascinating history.

DID THE SPOKANE POLICE DEPARTMENT HAVE STICKY FINGERS?

One of the reasons the Spokane Police Department would turn a blind eye to the houses of ill repute is that they were a source of good, consistent revenue for the city. The women would pay a monthly fine of fifteen dollars on the first of each month to ply their trade. In 1910, there were 125 (recorded) prostitutes working on Front Avenue in Spokane. Each woman would pay her fine and continue working the remainder of the month without trouble or arrests from the police.

But in the summer of 1910, things got a little fishy. The city treasurer (among other officials) was suspected of having sticky fingers. The numbers didn't add up, and these officials were caught red handed. Someone noted that in June, the collected fines only came to $87, but $15 times 125 soiled doves should have amounted to $1,875 in revenue for that month. So where did the other $1,788 go?

Earlier, in 1904, the police department had been caught doing something strange. It was the job of the police department to make sure all businesses had valid licenses to work, per ordinance #477. Yet for some odd reason, licensing for the huge collection of psychics working in Spokane was never enforced.

In 1904, there were over 150 psychics, palmists, clairvoyants and trance mediums working within the city limits. These fortunetellers lined the streets, luring in any person who felt they needed help and reassurance from the afterlife. The typical scam was charging two dollars to read a person's palm and then assuring them that for another ten dollars, the psychic could go into a trance and speak directly to their deceased loved ones.

Spokane licenses cost $200 per year per business. This would have promised the city $30,000 in licensing fees from the physics. It would have paid for the police department's salaries and even had some money left over.

So why was Chief Waller not enforcing ordinance #477 from this particular group of businesses? No one ever knew. Perhaps Waller was paranoid of dark curses that could be placed on him by certain individuals.

SPOKANE'S MAIL CLERK SCANDAL

Glenn Boughton was a very young mail clerk working in Spokane at the post office during the summer of 1910. He had been married just one week when he decided to chance his luck. When the very tempting registered letter containing $2,000 came sliding across his front counter, he casually slipped the envelope off to one side and hoped no one would notice.

After his shift was done, he went to the train station and bought tickets for him and his wife, heading off to Minneapolis, where his parents lived. He was going to start a new life with his bride and his pockets full of cash.

But as they were boarding the train, a police officer blocked him and arrested him on charges of embezzlement.

Upon questioning Boughton, they discovered that earlier that year in April, he had also stolen a large packet of money that he claimed had "disappeared." He promptly went to prison when the federal grand jury found him guilty of the charges.

His new bride would have to wait five years before spending any quality time with her new husband.

LYRIC THEATER BOMBED

By the 1920s, Spokane had fourteen moving picture theaters to entertain citizens and tourists alike. One of the local favorite picture houses was the Lyric Theater, located in the Lindelle Building at 10 North Washington Street.

Jack Allender of Spokane bought eight theaters in and around Spokane, which gave him a great advantage in the entertainment industry. In 1915, he purchased the Lyric, and in 1918, he bought the Majestic Theater, which could hold 470 patrons.

Around midnight on July 6, 1928, Officer Henry Morris was doing his rounds. As he walked past the Lyric, he paused to see what shows were being offered. He took mental note of the times and shows and went along his merry way. He was not more than a few steps past the Lyric's entrance when he heard a loud *kaboooom!*

The entire ticket booth and the projection room were both blasted to smithereens by a homemade bomb. Debris was tossed high into the air and into the street. Luckily, no one was injured. Morris could have been killed.

The southeast corner of Riverside Avenue and Washington Street, Nichols and Granite Blocks, after the big fire of 1889. The stores on the left are Pacific Saddle Company, Buckler Grocery and the Vienna Bakery. *Courtesy of Spokane Public Library, Teakle Collection, Northwest Room.*

The Lyric never reopened as a theater, and the bombers were never captured.

In 1932, the building became a church. In 1948, it was turned into a military surplus store. In 1963, the building was turned over to the city, which promptly razed it, and the Lyric Theater became only a memory. In 1970, it became a parking lot.

A few years later, the Casino Theater also experienced a bombing. This time, the assailants used gas bombs and were captured by the police. Several angry union members—Al Edwards, Leo Cortesy and Robert McConahey— were found guilty and fined seventy-five dollars each. A cashier, Eva Jury, became the heroine when she tipped off the police. Perhaps these men also bombed the Lyric, but they never confessed to that one.

Dancing on Sundays and Wild Orgies!

All Sunday dancing positively must cease in Spokane. Nobody but a lot of hoodlums will commit sacrilege and defame the Lord's Day by dancing!
—*Spokane chief of police Leroy Waller, June 2, 1906*

Probably one of the most bizarre rules put into effect for Spokane citizens was that absolutely NO dancing would be permitted past midnight on Saturday, and anyone participating in this practice would be arrested. Unfortunately, much like the Prohibition law, it really only made people want to do it more.

One particular individual openly and actively defied the law. His name was Professor James Wilson. He felt the law was insane and decided to push his rights to the limit. Another professor, Professor Graham, joined the fun.

Wilson was originally from Seattle, Washington, where he ran a dance "academy" called the Ranke on the corner of Fifth and Pike Streets. There, he sleazily lured young girls into prostitution. He was soon kicked out of Seattle and left in a huff, leaving many bills unpaid.

Wilson made his way to the wild city of Spokane in 1906 and opened a new dance "academy" named the Olympia Dance Hall on the corner of First Avenue and Stevens Street. He claimed, "Anything and everything is allowed here and anyone, regardless of character, was welcome if he had the price of admission!" The price was fifty cents to enter the Olympia for a wild night of debauchery. Women and girls were allowed in for free, of course.

Wilson soon became known as the "Dance Impresario of Spokane." Talk of wild parties, illegal and underage drinking, sinful sex with young girls and much more began to surface. Chief Waller was beside himself and stated, "There will be clean dancing or all the names of participants will be publicly published!" What the chief didn't realize is that most of the indecent dancers couldn't have cared less. They were having way too much fun!

The Olympia began getting a lot of heat and hassle from the police. So Wilson decided to be proactive and move his academy elsewhere. Soon, his "classes" were located at Turner Hall at 25 Third Street in town. Wilson himself printed flyers announcing the opening of his new academy and handed them out to all the people still hanging out at the Olympia. He also rounded up some prostitutes from Spokane's tenderloin district, inviting them to come join the fun. He even made his new space more enticing by stamping the ticket so people could reenter for free, thus allowing them to come and go as they pleased, taking libations at nearby pubs and saloons and then returning to Turner Hall to "dance."

Waller was red in the face and claimed, "I will raid every dance that Wilson orchestrates!"

Professor Graham began his own Sunday dances at the nearby Elks Temple. These, too, were considered indecent and unlawful and in defiance of the law. The dancing and sinning would go on all night, and precisely at

In 1920, Internal Revenue chemist G.F. Beyer examines a confiscated half-pint bottle someone bought for four dollars, but the seller had applied a one-quart stamp that he had steamed off another bottle. This sample actually contained water colored with burnt sugar. *Courtesy of the Library of Congress #2016827374 and Herbert A. French.*

midnight, the bell would strike, the lights would be turned off and all kinds of wickedness would ensue. This became termed the "Midnight Waltz," but in reality, it was an orgy.

Meanwhile, Graham's hall was also overflowing with sinners. He was having a ball and even invited policemen to join in on the fun. They would be allowed to "keep order" in his place. Officer Scott quickly volunteered for the job. But Scott soon forgot his orders and was thoroughly enjoying the attention he was receiving from the ladies.

All the Sunday dancing and orgies eventually lost their steam, and the chief got his way.

It is interesting to note that Professor Wilson later ran for a position on Spokane City Council in 1908. Perhaps he wanted to influence the city to have a little more fun!

Judge Caught Red-Handed!

Judge M.J. Gordon was the formal council attorney for the Great Northern Railroad living in Spokane. He was living life high on the hog—that is, until he got caught embezzling money in 1909.

His list of crimes was long, as he was becoming an expert at stealing funds. He casually did everything from passing bad checks to misappropriating funds into his personal bank account. When the Great Northern Railroad trusted him with $9,200 that was to go to the family of James Sparrow (a mail clerk who had died in a train accident in 1907), he secretly kept the money. When he stole Great Northern's $28,000 in Stevens County tax money, he didn't think he would get caught. When Great Northern's books were audited and showed a $60,000 to $75,000 shortage, he didn't think he would get caught. When he stole $3,500 and another $12,500 of Great Northern's money that was set aside for the judgments against the railroad in the case of the Frost-Cope Lumber Company against the railroad, he didn't think he would get caught.

When Sheriff Clarence Long demanded a grand jury investigation by the City of Spokane into Gordon's activity, Gordon demanded, "I am innocent!" Eventually, the case against Gordon was dismissed, leaving the citizens of Spokane shaking their heads.

A COLD WAR MISSILE LAUNCH SITE TURNED MURDER SITE TURNED UFO REPORTING CENTER

One of the craziest parcels in Washington lies just outside Spokane. It was part of nine sites used for underground missiles for Fairforce Airforce Base 567th Squadron in 1960. The bases are scattered around eastern Washington. These now-empty silos are mostly owned by private citizens. Spokane was once a hot target for the Soviet Union during the Cold War. Each of these silos was about eighteen thousand square feet of underground facility, and the 3.75-megaton ballistic missiles were positioned upright (the launch container was called the Coffin), not horizontally, as typical. They were aimed specifically at the Soviet Union, and rumors suggest that one time they were stopped just fifteen minutes prior to launch. Each site could withstand an atomic blast that was fifty times larger than Hiroshima. Each base cost $4 million to construct.

In 1965, the missiles were removed, and the sites became abandoned.

Site Atlas #6 and its twenty-two acres was sold in 1988 as a private residence to a long-haul truck driver named Ralph Benson. He only paid $32,500 for the multimillion-dollar site. He lived in the creepy, gigantic shelter until 2002.

On June 12, 2002, a Washington State fuel tax auditor, Roger Erdman, had an appointment with Benson. The audit was random, but Benson panicked. He knew he owed the state $6,000 in unpaid fuel taxes. Erdman was simply doing his job, as Benson had recently filed bankruptcy. Erdman had no idea he would never be seen alive again.

Benson shot Erdman in the back of the head and then dismembered his body, tossing the pieces in a ditch forty miles away. Benson was quickly arrested, as hundreds of pieces of evidence securing his guilt were recovered by the police from Atlas #6. Although he pleaded not guilty, Benson was convicted and sent to Monroe State Reformatory, north of Seattle.

Police became suspicious of another possible murder. They discovered that the stolen truck of another long-haul driver named John Deetz was found on a parcel Benson owned in California. Deetz had gone missing in 1988; he was last seen several days after Christmas. Benson was never formally charged with Deetz's disappearance, as there was not enough evidence. The police also suspected Benson of multiple crimes committed from Texas all the way to Nevada.

Benson died in prison in 2004.

In 2006, Atlas #6 was sold again. Peter Davenport, a graduate of both Stanford University and Washington State University, purchased the unusual site as a home base for his large collection of UFO reports (over ninety thousand). Davenport is the founder of the National UFO Reporting Center (www.UFOcenter.com) and has been for almost three decades. He continues his research and occasionally gives tours to curious sightseers.

The strange history of Atlas #6, from nuclear missile bunker to house of horrors to UFO center, makes it one of the weirdest and wickedest spots near Spokane.

TEENAGE DAREDEVIL PILOT TAKES HIS FINAL FLIGHT IN SPOKANE

Sometimes wicked and crazy things can be a good thing. Like being wickedly *brave*! This is the case of the youngest pilot in United States history. A boy named Cromwell Dixon was born in San Francisco on July 9, 1892. Little did his mother know at the time that Cromwell would evolve into one of the most well-loved aviators in history.

Cromwell was an inventive genius with remarkable mechanic skills. At age ten, he built a boat with a homemade gas motor. In 1907, at age fifteen, he invented what he called a "skycycle," a combination of a hot air balloon and a bicycle. He took an old bike and removed its wheels

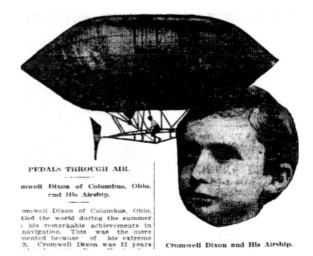

Young aviator Cromwell Dixon, who, in 1907 at age fifteen, invented what he called a "skycycle." *Courtesy of* Topeka State Journal, *December 7, 1907.*

PEDALS THROUGH AIR.

mwell Dixon of Columbus, Ohio, and His Airship.

omwell Dixon of Columbus, Ohio, tied the world during the summer his remarkable achievements in navigation. This was the more mented because of his extreme h. Cromwell Dixon was 12 years

Cromwell Dixon and His Airship.

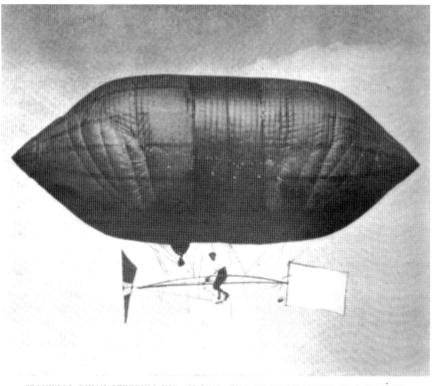

CROMWELL DIXON STEERING HIS AIR-SHIP, THE *MOON*, BY MEANS OF A BICYCLE
ARRANGEMENT.

Above: Dixon's skycycle was a combination between a hot air balloon and a bicycle. His mother took to sewing the 450 yards of Japanese silk together to make the balloon. *Courtesy of the* Ohio State Journal, *October 24, 1912, Columbus Metropolitan Library.*

Left: Cromwell Dixon died tragically in an accident at Spokane while getting ready to perform his "Dixon Corkscrew" on October 2, 1911, at the early age of nineteen. *Courtesy of the* Perth Amboy Evening News, *October 4, 1911.*

and forks. He made a two-blade silk propeller and rudder with a bamboo frame. He then attached the bike to the balloon and controlled the rudder with ropes attached to the handlebars. His mother took to sewing the 450 yards of Japanese silk together to make the balloon, finished off with a layer of varnish. He made his own generator to fill the thirty-two-foot-long balloon with hydrogen gas.

Cromwell flew his skycycle all over the place gathering great attention and affection from the locals. Soon, he was in the newspapers with his daring creation. He entered the balloon race called the Gordon Bennett Cup at age fourteen and became the first person to cross the Mississippi River. This feat took him thirty minutes of air time. His frantic and worried mother yelled to her son from the land below, "Cromwell, don't you *dare* cross that river!"

The young pilot just smiled at his mother and called back, "Catch me if you can, Mama!"

In 1911, Cromwell earned his pilot license (number 43) and became the youngest pilot in the United States. He was also the first person to fly over the Continental Divide, earning him $10,000 cash. (The money was fronted by Louis Hill of the Great Northern Railroad and John Ringling of the circus, as well as a few others.) No pilot had successfully flown this path, and all who had tried ended up dying. He achieved this feat with his new Curtiss biplane (that he named *Hummingbird*) and garnered even more admiration. He secured a contract with the Interstate Fair in Spokane to do three airshows a day. His signature move was called the "Dixon Corkscrew," and everyone who saw his downward plunge trick held their breath in both fear and awe.

But young Cromwell's luck was about to change. On October 2, 1911, at age nineteen, Cromwell was to take his very last flight.

A strong wind flipped his biplane, and he was unable to control it. The *Hummingbird* came falling from the sky from one hundred feet up in front of twelve thousand spectators. Horrified people watched in shock as they saw his plane descend to the land below at an alarming rate.

"Here I go! Here I go!" he was heard screaming.

Help arrived at the crash site, but poor Cromwell was in bad shape. His face was smashed, his right leg broken and his collarbone shattered. He was rushed to the nearest hospital, unconscious.

Unfortunately, he died of a severe concussion and brain hemorrhage just an hour after the accident. Spokane citizens and tourists were devastated, as were all Americans. They had lost their brave and handsome hero. His body was shipped back to New York, where his mother was living at the time.

He had told reporters on October 3, 1911, "If I have an accident in the air, I hope that it will come when I am so high that I will be dead before I reach the ground."

Unfortunately, that was not the case.

His mother told reporters, "My boy's one ambition in life was to become an aviator and he devoted his whole time to it for years. When he was 12 he started to navigate his skycycle near our home in Columbus, Ohio. There was nothing but bravery in my boy. In spite of the dangers in his hazardous work, he tried and tried until he was successful."

Cromwell Dixon is remembered by Spokane citizens and by the world as the bravest boy in aviator history. His tragic death still inspires sorrow in anyone who discovers his story. Some people thought he was crazy; others knew he was a genius. One can only imagine the accomplishments Cromwell would have achieved if he had lived a full life.

WASHINGTON'S BIGGEST BANK HEIST: THE DISHMAN STATE BANK ROBBERY IN SPOKANE

A handsome twenty-one-year-old man decided he wanted to make a life of crime. He was on his way, as he had been committing countless burglaries and car thefts for years. His dream was to become famous like his heroes, gangster such as John Dillinger or George "Pretty Boy" Floyd.

On September 10, 1954, George Quatsling decided to hold up the Dishman State Bank located at 8412 East Sprague Avenue in Spokane. He somehow managed to sneak into the bank before it opened, so when the bank manager and the other twelve employees began to arrive that morning, Quatsling casually and politely led them to a back room. When all the employees were accounted for, he brought out bank manager Glen Harrington and requested he open the vault. Nervously, Harrington succeeded but was unable to remove the wire cage. Frustrated, Quatsling forced the cage apart with a screwdriver.

He began filling up a paper sack with the stolen money, and when that broke, he grabbed a cardboard box and started stuffing that with the cash. When he was happy with his loot, he pushed everyone back into the room, cut the telephone lines and locked the door. He then made his getaway in a red car. A witness across the street saw him drive off. He had grabbed $136,000 in cash.

The next day, a man named Tillie Mely called the police with a tip. He told the cops that his new neighbor was out painting a red car in the middle of the night using only a small flashlight to assist him. He found that *very* odd. So did the police.

Officers Alfred Stoser and Menzo Clinton arrived at Quatsling's home and knocked on his door. The suspect answered. When he was asked to allow them to search the place, he agreed. As Clinton was in another room, Stoser looked in the bathroom. Quatsling followed him, pointed a gun in his face and said, "Don't move or I will kill you!"

Stoser wasn't frightened by the young man. Instead, he knocked the weapon from his hand and smashed him into the bathtub, then handcuffed him. Quatsling was restrained while they searched his house. Under the bed, they found a suitcase full of cash, forty-two guns, fifteen rifles and a bunch of ammunition.

He was promptly taken to the Spokane County Jail. The officers discovered that Quatsling had escaped from Jefferson County prison in Golden, Colorado, and had a rap sheet a mile long.

After his trial, he was sentenced to ten years in McNeil Island Federal Penitentiary but then moved to Alcatraz to become inmate #1177.

The Dishman Bandit did gather some fame, as he had almost gotten away with the biggest robbery in Washington State (at that time).

TRAIN ROBBERS WANTED—DEAD OR ALIVE!

In 1909, a group of train robbers were terrorizing the railroads from the Dakotas, through Spokane, all the way to the West Coast. The bandits were ruthless and seemed impossible to catch.

By May, the railroad companies, the United States Postal Service and the detectives had had enough. A whopping reward of $86,000 ($2,397,697.20 in today's money) was posted in the hopes that someone would be able to put an end to this nonsense. They suspected four to six men were involved in the robberies. Great Northern Railroad ponied up $60,000 toward the reward of the four bandits, the postal service $6,000—and then another $20,000 if the other two suspects were captured. The reward was valid whether the men were brought in dead or alive. Of course, it had to be proven that the men captured were actually the train robbers, or else people would just be killing their enemies and pretending they were the bandits to get the reward money.

Many cowboys would ambush a train in order to rob it of its cash and valuables. The Pinkerton Detectives were always hot on their trail. *Courtesy of W.D. Harper in 1904 and the Library of Congress #2014647414.*

On Saturday night, May 16, 1909, one of the most merciless robberies was committed, risking the lives of over a dozen innocent passengers and employees. Just outside Spokane, as the train was pulling away and gathering steam, Great Northern train no. 3 was heading west. Suddenly, around 1:00 a.m., four men rode up on their horses, jumped aboard and waved their guns around yelling, "Hands up, we'll shoot!"

Then they expertly unhooked the fast mail car engine and pulled it away from the passenger coach. The terrorized mail clerk had a gun pointed at his head and was ordered to open the safe that held all the certified mail and money. The railroad crew was on guard, as this would be the second robbery near Hillyard in a month. Fireman John Hall and engineer William Miller, the only two railroad employees on board, were terrified. They were told to get off the train.

As the bandits were rifling through the mail, cherry picking out the money, passengers were relieved that they were safe from harm.

But they weren't.

After the robbers emptied the safe of approximately $20,000, their ruthless deed was not completed. They put the engine in reverse. The conductor on the passenger coach soon saw that the mail engine was being returned to them, coming down the tracks at twenty-five miles per hour heading straight at them. If the train wasn't stopped, it could kill all the innocent passengers.

Hurriedly, the remaining crew members began moving nearby railroad ties and logs over the tracks—anything they could do to slow down the oncoming train. The brakeman aboard tried to slow down the train but was unable. The engine slammed into the coach, causing a huge crash, and all the windows shattered onto the twelve passengers. Everyone on the coach barely escaped death.

Detectives were determined to find the bandits before they could cause any more harm or rob any more trains. All were on high alert, from Minnesota to the Dakotas all the way to the West Coast. Some of the suspects were a man known as McDonald and another named Ed Frankhouser. They had been implicated in a robbery in Rondo Siding, Montana, in 1907.

Eventually other men—W.D. Woods, Fred Tortenson and James Gordon—were arrested by Detective Alexander McDonald for the

Two unidentified cowhands and a horse relaxing on a fence at a Spokane ranch. *Courtesy of John Vachon, Beaverhead County United States Montana Spokane Ranch, Library of Congress #2017814967.*

robbery just outside Spokane. Once in jail, officers discovered that Woods was really Dan Downer, a known horse thief. The other two men were also horse thieves, wanted in Everett, Washington. Gordon's real name was Gordon "Red Shirt" Golden. All three men were known criminals in Spokane.

Woods and Gordon later escaped the Folsom State Prison.

It is unclear who eventually received the grand reward.

Crazy Lovesick Cowboy Tries to Kidnap Actress

A beautiful Spokane actress named Princess Amelio (real name Lena Espenwad) who entertained patrons at the Coeur d'Alene Theater in the city almost fell victim to being kidnapped.

It all started one hot night during the summer of 1907. A cowboy, known only as Jack, watched in awe as the lovely lady performed her act on stage. Jack immediately fell hopelessly in love with her. After the final curtain call, Jack was able to woo his way into her bed. The pair had an evening of passionate, mad sex, after which Jack was uncontrollable. He became obsessed with Lena and refused to take no for an answer. He began overwhelming her with flowers and gifts, hoping to win her heart.

But Lena had other plans. They may have had a fun evening, but she had no plans of getting entangled in a relationship, especially with a down-on-his-luck cowboy. All she really knew about him was that he worked at a ranch in Ephrata.

Over and over again, Jack begged Lena to marry him. Finally, she agreed just to get him off her back. Jack got back on his horse and headed back to Ephrata. Relieved, Lena thought that would be the end of it. But when Jack returned to inquire about their marriage plans, Lena had to tell him that she was just joking. The cowboy became infuriated and stormed off yelling, "I'm going to kill you!"

Frightened, Lena continued to watch over her shoulder for days.

One night, as Lena was walking to her apartment at the Monica Hotel after a show, two cowboys raced up to her. She stood startled on the corner of Front Avenue and Wall Street when she realized one of the cowboys was Jack. He said, "Well, sweetheart, it's all off. I am going back to the ranch. Let's shake hands."

Cowboys, like those in this group, roamed the land near Spokane and were eager to rob a train or a bank on a whim. *Courtesy of the Library of Congress #2006679142.*

As he extended his rough hand out for her to shake, Lena hesitantly offered her hand back. Just as quickly, Jack grabbed her arm and swung her up onto his horse. Jack and his friend spurred their horses and both took off down Wall Street.

Jack's horse was not used to skirts though, and as Lena's flapped in the wind, the horse became frightened and started bucking. Soon, both Lena and Jack were thrown to the ground, and Lena was kicked in her back. As she cried out in pain, onlookers rushed to her side. Jack remounted his steed, and the cowboys galloped off into the sunset.

Poor Lena was assisted back to her apartment at the Monica, where she was put to bed to rest. She was anxious and was worried her assailants would return to try to kidnap her again. When the doctor examined her, she had a dark bruise in the shape of a horseshoe on her back.

In the morning, against her physician's suggestions, she boarded a train heading to Idaho to hide out.

Jack and Lena were never seen again in Spokane.

GAMBLER LEAPS TO HIS DEATH
FROM MONROE STREET BRIDGE

William "Bud" Armstrong was a well-known faro dealer at the Combination Saloon in Spokane. Well mannered and friendly, he was a longtime friend of the saloon's owner, R.W. Woods.

Armstrong had been living with a woman in room 17 at the Savoy Hotel on Main Avenue and Howard Street. He became hopelessly addicted to morphine and had to be placed in the Lidgerwood Sanitarium for mental issues. The night before his death, he escaped the insane asylum by crawling out the kitchen window. People frantically searched for him all night.

About 6:45 a.m., Woods was in front of the Combination getting ready to open for the day when he spotted his old buddy driving by in a car. When he hollered out to his friend, Armstrong simply smiled and waved.

Just ten minutes later, Armstrong would be dead.

At the Monroe Street Bridge, Armstrong got out of the car and walked to the middle of the bridge, where he removed his hat and watch, placing them gently on the street. Two men, J.H. Mower and B.D. Pace, who were riding their bikes, were curious what Armstrong was doing. Once they realized that he was planning on jumping off the bridge, they ran to his aid. By the time they got to Armstrong, he had already crawled over the guardrail and was hanging on the ledge. When Mower and Pace tried to help Armstrong, he simply grinned and let go. Many people watched in horror as Armstrong fell 146 feet to his death, landing on the rocks below.

The police siren was alarmed, and soon Officers Buckholz and Lewis arrived at the bloody scene, along with Coroner Smith.

Woods told the police, "I knew him in Spokane before the Northern Pacific Railroad was built in town. He was never married, and if he had any family, I never heard him speak of them."

The unidentified woman Armstrong was living with at the Savoy disappeared without a trace.

BIBLIOGRAPHY

Articles

Albuquerque Morning Journal (NM). "Train Robberies." June 4, 1909.

Arksey, Laura. "Prohibition: Booze Routes to Spokane." March 9, 2011. HistoryLink.org, essay 9702.

Atlanta Georgian (GA). "F. Lewis Clark Missing." February 3, 1914.

Bismarck Daily Tribune (ND). "F. Lewis Clark Missing." February 20, 1914.

———. "Robert Landis Story." November 15, 1929.

Blecha, Peter. "Durkin, James (1859–1934) Prohibition." June 21, 2009. HistoryLink.org, essay 9018.

———. "Tipton, Billy (1914–1989)." September 17, 2005. HistoryLink. org, essay 7456.

Bliesner, Josh. "The Death of Cromwell Dixon: A Daring Aviator Meets a Tragic End." Spokane Historical. spokanehistorical.org/items/show/531.

Boardman, Mark. "Butch Cassidy Wannabe: The Strange Tale of Butch Phillips." *True West Magazine*, January 10, 2012.

Boston Globe. "F. Lewis Clark Missing." February 23, 1929.

Brand, Nathan. "Hidden Spokane: Exploring an Underground Maze." KREM.com. www.krem.com/article/entertainment/places/hidden-spokane/hidden-spokane-exploring-an-underground-maze/293-123275737.

———. "Unsolved Secrets of Lost Spokane: Episode 1." November 28, 2013. www.youtube.com/watch?v=tceA_MaseXI.

Camporeale, Logan. "Dynamite Blast Wrecks Lyric Theatre." Spokane Historical. spokanehistorical.org/items/show/631.

Cohen, Zach C. "Did Butch Cassidy Survive? Uncovered Manuscript Says He Died of Old Age." *Time*, August 16, 2011.

Corrigan, Mike. "Speakeasy Spelunking." Inlander, February 12, 2001. www.inlander.com/spokane/speakeasy-spelunking/Content?oid=2173400.

Daily Capital Journal (Salem, OR). "F. Lewis Clark Missing." June 2, 1914.

Daily Missoulian (Missoula, MT). "Cromwell Dixon Stories." October 3, 1911.

———. "F. Lewis Clark Missing." January 18, 1914.

Dakota Farmers Leader (Canton, SD). "Train Robberies." May 21, 1909.

Detroit Times (MI). "Carrie Nation Stories." January 18, 1911.

Dufton, Emily. "Politics & Poison: Government Sanctioned Murder During Prohibition." Points History, May 17, 2016. pointshistory.com/2016/05/17/politics-poison-government-sanctioned-murder-during-prohibition/#more-14388.

Evening Capital News (Boise, ID). "F. Lewis Clark Missing." June 16, 1914.

Evening Statesman. "Stotko Murder." December 9, 1907.

Geranios, Nicholas K. "Benson Murders: Detectives Say Trucker May Have Killed Before." *Seattle Times*, January 1, 2004.

Kendrick Gazette (ID). "Mail Clerk Fraud." June 10, 1910.

Kershner, Jim. "Man Who Wrote Butch Cassidy Died in Spokane Changes Story." *Spokesman-Review*, July 22, 2012.

———. "Spokane Neighborhoods: Old Chinatown—Trent Alley—Thumbnail History." March 30, 2007. HistoryLink.org, essay 8120.

Lake County Times (Hammond, IN). June 23, 1911.

Lambeth, Robert M. "The Murder of Officer Robert J. Rusk." Spokane Historical. spokanehistorical.org/items/show/556.

McClary, Daryl C. "Henry Arao Murders Tailor Sam Chow in Spokane on December 29, 1904." December 28, 2011. HistoryLink.org, essay 9993.

Pensacola Journal (FL). "F. Lewis Clark Missing." January 20, 1914.

Perth Amboy Evening News (NJ). "Cromwell Dixon Crash." October 3, 1911.

Prohibition: An Interactive History. "The Speakeasies of the 1920s." prohibition.themobmuseum.org/the-history/the-prohibition-underworld/the-speakeasies-of-the-1920s.

Raleigh, Jason. "The Enduring Mystery of F. Lewis Clark." *The Ouija Broads* podcast, January 21, 2019. www.ouijabroads.com/guides/2019/1/21/the-mysterious-disappearance-of-f-lewis-clark.

Reames, Nicolette. "Spokane's Chinatown," Spokane Historical. spokanehistorical.org/items/show/400.

River Press (Fort Benton, MT). "Cromwell Dixon Stories." October 11, 1911.

Roundup (Record, MT). "Cromwell Dixon Stories." October 6, 1911.

Salt Lake City Herald (UT). Lynch murder information. October 13, 1903; October 15, 1903; October 19, 1903; January 9, 1907.

Seattle Star. "Stotko Murder." August 17, 1907.

Shain, Caitlin M. "The Death of 'Irish Kate.'" Spokane Historical. spokanehistorical.org/items/show/456.

Spokane Press. "Armstrong Suicide." April 9, 1903.

———. "Bomb in Theatre." July 6, 1928.

———. "Calamity Jane in Spokane." August 6, 1903; October 21, 1908; August 5, 1910.

———. "Carrie Nation Stories." May 2, 1910.

———. "Charles Kemp Murder." December 28, 1909.

———. "Chinatown Information." January 9, 1903; January 28, 1904.

———. "Christmas Murder." December 25, 1909.

———. "Cowboy Grabs Actress." July 8, 1907.

———. "Cromwell Dixon Stories." October 21, 1907.

———. "Dora Falk." December 13, 1910; December 20, 1910; December 27, 1910.

———. "Edward Krause Murder." April 13, 1910.

———. "E.P. Fulton Story." March 7, 1906.

———. "Found Jewels." September 4, 1909.

———. "14 Robberies in 10 Days." October 15, 1910.

———. "French Sex Slaves." August 13, 1903; August 18, 1903; August 22, 1907; January 19, 1909; October 18, 1909.

———. "Gambling Raids." November 2, 1904; November 12, 1904; July 3, 1909; June 2, 1910.

———. "Gouyet Brother Stories." July 3, 1903; July 13, 1908; October 12, 1908; October 19, 1908.

———. "Great Northern Train Robberies." May 17, 1909; May 22, 1909; July 21, 1909.

———. "Henry Arao Kills Chow." December 29, 1904.

———. "Huck Narrowly Escapes Death." January 23, 1909.

———. "Ill Repute Scandals." September 14, 1903; April 14, 1904; April 12, 1910; June 22, 1910.

———. "James Coverly Story." March 13, 1905.

———. "James Degnin Suicide." February 20, 1903.

———. "Judge Embezzlement/Gordon-Root Scandal." November 30, 1908; January 21, 1909; April 24, 1909; May 6, 1909; March 10, 1910.

———. "Lloyd Bar Murder." December 28, 1909; March 18, 1910; April 8, 1910; April 13, 1910; April 25, 1910.

———. "Lynch Murder Stories." October 13, 1903.

———. "Mail Clerk Fraud." June 3, 1910.

———. "Mayor Says Burns Lied." October 4, 1904.

———. "McDonald Train Robbery." October 28, 1907.

———. "Minister Tells Father to Kill." December 23, 1904; January 7, 1905; January 14, 1905.

———. "Most Brutal Hold Up." March 17, 1906.

———. "Murder of a Baby." September 20, 1904; September 21, 1904; September 22, 1904.

———. "No Dancing and Orgies." March 24, 1906; March 26, 1906; March 28, 1906; July 2, 1906; May 13, 1907; May 15, 1907.

———. "Opium and Noodle Joints." September 19, 1904; September 10, 1906; September 15, 1906; July 11, 1910.

———. "Police Corruption." November 18, 1904.

———. "Prohibition Stories." August 2, 1907; May 12, 1910.

———. "Prostitution Stories." October 27, 1903; April 25, 1904; August 26, 1907; September 7, 1907; July 13, 1908; October 28, 1908; July 15, 1910; October 28, 1907; July 27, 1910.

———. "Roy Fordyce Murder." December 29, 1910; January 2, 1930.

———. "Sidney Sloane Stories." December 12, 1906.

———. "Slashed His Throat Then Shot Himself." March 13, 1905.

———. "Society Man in Spokane." November 15, 1902.

———. "Spokane Facts." January 3, 1910; May 11, 1910.

———. "Stack Boy Murder." July 3, 1903.

———. "Stotko Murder." April 4, 1905; April 5, 1905; April 6, 1905; April 7, 1905; November 11, 1905; August 17, 1907; October 5, 1907; February 26, 1908; November 24, 1908.

———. "Y.M.C.A. Murder of Hutchinson." October 16, 1906; October 17, 1906; October 22, 1906; October 18, 1906; October 19, 1906; March 13, 1907; November 6, 1908.

Spokesman Review. "Prohibition Closures." December 18, 1927.

———. "Robbery of Sing Fat." November 30, 1913.

St. Mary Banner (Franklin, IA). "Cromwell Dixon Stories." January 11, 1908.

Stockton Independent (CA). "Train Robberies." May 16, 1909.

Topeka State Journal (KS). "Cromwell Dixon Stories." December 7, 1907.

Unsolved Mysteries. "Butch Cassidy." unsolvedmysteries.fandom.com/wiki/Butch_Cassidy.

Ward, Scott. "The Death of Bill Jackson: Police Brutality or Rough Justice?" Spokane Historical. spokanehistorical.org/items/show/741.

Wikipedia. "Butch Cassidy." en.wikipedia.org/wiki/Butch_Cassidy.

———. "Prohibition in the United States." en.wikipedia.org/wiki/Prohibition_in_the_United_States#Medical_liquor.

Websites

www.ancestry.com.

www.findagrave.com.

www.historylink.org.

www.libraryofcongress.org.

www.wikimedia.org.

ABOUT THE AUTHOR

*O*riginally from upstate New York, Deborah Cuyle loves everything about the history of her favorite cities that she has lived in or loves. Her passions include local history, animals, museums, rock hunting and horseback riding. She, her husband and her son are currently remodeling a historic, crumbling mansion in Milbank, South Dakota, built in 1883.

Visit us at
www.historypress.com